MAJORS-ONLY DECK

PISTIS SOPHIA
The Goddess Tarot

Kim Huggens and Nic Phillips

4880 Lower Valley Road, Atglen, PA 19310

Copyright © 2020 by Kim Huggens & Nic Phillips

Library of Congress Control Number: 2020930562

All rights reserved. No part of this work may be reproduced or used in any form or by any means—graphic, electronic, or mechanical, including photocopying or information storage and retrieval systems—without written permission from the publisher.

The scanning, uploading, and distribution of this book or any part thereof via the Internet or any other means without the permission of the publisher is illegal and punishable by law. Please purchase only authorized editions and do not participate in or encourage the electronic piracy of copyrighted materials.

"Red Feather Mind Body Spirit" logo is a trademark of Schiffer Publishing, Ltd.
"Red Feather Mind Body Spirit Feather" logo is a registered trademark of Schiffer Publishing, Ltd.

Type set in Adorn Copperplate/Agenda/Minion
ISBN: 978-0-7643-6001-5
Printed in China

Published by Red Feather Mind, Body, Spirit
An imprint of Schiffer Publishing, Ltd.
4880 Lower Valley Road
Atglen, PA 19310
Phone: (610) 593-1777; Fax: (610) 593-2002
E-mail: Info@schifferbooks.com
Web: www.redfeathermbs.com

For our complete selection of fine books on this and related subjects, please visit our website at www.schifferbooks.com. You may also write for a free catalog.

Schiffer Publishing's titles are available at special discounts for bulk purchases for sales promotions or premiums. Special editions, including personalized covers, corporate imprints, and excerpts, can be created in large quantities for special needs. For more information, contact the publisher.

We are always looking for people to write books on new and related subjects. If you have an idea for a book, please contact us at proposals@schifferbooks.com.

KIM

For Evelyn and Myles.
May their lives be filled with
other people's myths.

NIC

To the seeker: Do not forsake wisdom, and she will protect you;
love her, and she will watch over you.

ACKNOWLEDGMENTS

This deck's journey from the beginning of its creation to the end has been long, and a lifetime seems to have passed in those twelve years. We both have been blessed with each other's friendship along the way, with *Pistis Sophia: The Goddess Tarot* running as an undercurrent through our growing, changing lives. Now that it is done, we know that memory cannot do justice to every individual who has helped us along the way with encouragement, book recommendations, poses for cards, and suggestions. Not all of those who began this journey by our sides are still with us, but we remember them fondly.

Kim would like to thank her Mum and Dad—Eileen and Bill—who gave her courage and taught her that nothing worth doing was ever easy. Although her Dad has passed, his memory has driven her on, helping her push through the most exhausting and difficult parts of the journey. She would also like to thank her friends Chrissy Derbyshire, David Benton, Sarah Fisher, and Simon Lewis for all their suggestions and input about the stories and figures in the deck. She owes thanks to her Vodou *fanmi*, her *sosyete*—Sosyete Gade Nou Leve—and Papa Hector Salva for all their love and teaching. Finally, she wishes to thank Alex Brown for his complete faith in her and for fighting by her side these several years.

Nic would like to thank his parents—Paul and Margaret—for their love and support, and from whom he gained his interest in the unseen. To all the friends already mentioned by Kim, for their input over the years and for those in the online community who have patiently waited for the follow-up to our first deck, giving us encouragement and enthusiasm throughout *Pistis Sophia*'s creation. To Matthew Arathoon for his unconditional support and faith in me, and Binah Puss for her unconditional kitty cuddles on many a night sat in front of the PC and drawing board.

CONTENTS

Introduction 6
Getting Started on the Tarot Path 13
Reading with *Pistis Sophia: The Goddess Tarot* 18
Tarot Spreads with *Pistis Sophia: The Goddess Tarot* 20
Card Meanings 30

0 The Fool 32
I The Magician 37
II The High Priestess 42
III The Empress 47
IV The Construct 52
V The Hierophant 56
VI The Sisters 60
VII The Chariot 65
VIII Strength 69
IX The Hermit 74
X The Wheel of Fortune 78
XI Justice 83
XII The Mystic 88
XIII Death 93
XIV Alchemy 97
XV The Devil 101
XVI The Tower 106
XVII The Star 110
XVIII The Moon 114
XIX The Sun 120
XX Rebirth 124
XXI The Universe 128

Bibliography 134

INTRODUCTION

Wisdom is sweeter than honey,

Brings more joy than wine,

Illumines more than the sun,

Is more precious than jewels.

She causes the ears to hear

And the heart to comprehend.

I love her like a Mother,

And she embraces me as her own child.

I will follow her footprints

And she will not cast me away.

attributed to Makeda, the Queen of Sheba,
ca. 1000 BCE. Quoted in Hirshfield 1994, 13.

Why Another Goddess Tarot?

There are a number of goddess Tarot and oracle decks already available. This may raise the question of the usefulness of another goddess Tarot when so many already fill this niche. Readers familiar with our previous deck, *Sol Invictus: The God Tarot*, may also question our creation of a goddess Tarot, given that in that deck we said there were too many goddess decks and not a single god Tarot to provide the balance. It has been over a decade since the publication of *Sol Invictus: The God Tarot*, and the Tarot world has not changed much.

Nic and I were eager to continue creating and wished to personally explore the divine feminine, having already explored the divine masculine. *Pistis Sophia: The Goddess Tarot* became a personal journey of spiritual integration and understanding. We also wished to offer to those who enjoyed *Sol Invictus: The God Tarot* a goddess deck that kept to the same structure, art style, and level of research—this, we hoped, would enable lovers of the *God Tarot* to have a more complete experience of balance and integration themselves. It also became clear that some goddess decks are aimed solely at women, excluding prospective male users.

While, for convenience's sake, we often use the term "divine feminine" in this deck, we do not assume that all the goddesses herein are merely faces of one "universal goddess." Hard polytheists will be pleased to find that, instead, we have strived to show each individual goddess in her own right, with her own unique story, symbols, worship, hymns, and appearance. While we also recognize that many of the goddesses in this deck fit into archetypes that are repeated throughout mythology and history, we do not believe this necessitates a view that they are all a universal goddess. Rather, we wish to view each goddess as she was viewed by those who originally worshipped her, or in the case of some goddesses, by those who still worship her in living traditions.

As such, we have tried our best not to apply a worldview alien to the goddesses in each card. The only mindset with which we have approached these goddesses is that of the Tarot—and that only so we can apply the Tarot meanings to the myths, not to reshape the myths to fit our own agenda. Where possible, we return to the original sources of the goddesses we portray, using the original hymns and writings, as well as archeological sources, as the basis for our imagery and commentary.

We envisioned a goddess deck scholarly in its approach, which went to primary source material rather than relying on secondary commentaries, making further study for its readers all the more accessible, authentic, and exciting. So, in *Pistis Sophia: The Goddess Tarot*, we reunite the divine feminine with academia and the process of research. In many traditions of symbolism it is the divine masculine that is associated with logic and clear thought, while the divine feminine prevails in the creative, imaginative aspects of the mind. Here, we hope to enable the imagination and creativity of the reader by showing them, through our research and in a historically accurate way, what these beautiful, terrible, often profound, sometimes confusing goddesses are about.

Neolithic Goddesses and Unbroken Goddess Worship

It will become clear as one explores *Pistis Sophia: The Goddess Tarot* that there are no Neolithic "goddesses" to be found anywhere in the deck. The striking and evocative image of the Venus of Willendorf, for instance, does not find its way into the card imagery. This is not due to a lack of understanding of this time period, but instead due to the fact that these images are not conclusively goddesses: no records survive of their meaning to the people who owned their images; no remnants of ritual or oral tradition have been passed down. One possible interpretation of these figures is that they are representations of a mother goddess, worshipped from the earliest times and universally. A feminist reading of the archeological record asserts that these figures, alongside later ones such as those of Hellenistic times, indicate goddess worship in a matrilineal society that was later invaded and subsequently destroyed and oppressed by patriarchal cultures. Some scholars, such as Lotte Motz (1997), have suggested that these figures rarely show any signs of pregnancy or links to children or fertility, and that the idea of women's fertility as a profoundly sacred and worshipped aspect of human life is contrary to evidence from a vast array of ancient cultures. Motz concludes that these Neolithic "mother goddesses" are not what we have called them, and could be anything as simple as pretty pieces of artwork (Motz 1997, 5–23. For another examination of archeology relating to "The Goddess," see Goodison and Morris 1998, 6–21, and the chapter "Rethinking Figurines," 22–45).

Although we understand that a lack of evidence does not conclusively prove that these figures were *not* goddesses, it would be almost impossible to include them in *Pistis Sophia: The Goddess Tarot* as such. Although we do have female heroes and saints that aren't goddesses, they have their own myths, personalities, stories, rituals, and symbolism—something the Neolithic female figurines lack. In other words, we do not know what they originally meant to those who crafted them. We know nothing of their stories and did not want to transpose any modern interpretation onto them, when we have tried so rigorously to portray the other figures in the cards in their original meaning.

Women, Men, the Goddess, and Feminism

This is not just a deck for women. This is not just a deck for feminists. This is not just a deck for goddess worshippers. This is a deck simply for anybody—no matter their age, gender, religion, or view of the gods—to explore the divine feminine through the archetypes of the Tarot.

Both the *Goddess Tarot* and the *God Tarot* were created with the understanding and belief that physical gender is a vehicle in which the nongendered soul travels in this world. The *God Tarot* manifested its mysteries in the myths of male deities, and the *Goddess Tarot* in the myths of female deities, for two simple reasons: first, because it is convenient for us to see gendered beings in the cards, and second, to demonstrate the fact that whether a person or deity is male or female does not affect the personality traits, behaviors, and concepts that they experience and are associated with. (For a discussion of gender issues in modern spiritual practice, see Cruden 1995, 71–115.)

We also do not believe that divine feminine = woman. This is especially true when the idea of "maiden, mother, crone" is added to this, as it so often is not only in goddess decks but also Pagan decks. This symbol of the maiden, the mother, and the crone may be useful when looking at the phases of the moon, but it is lacking when applied to goddesses and women. Not all women choose to, or can, have children; defining women and their relation to the divine on the basis of their reproductive cycle is problematic. The same is true of many goddesses from various cultures: Not all of them fit neatly into this model of the goddess, and certainly not all of them are moon goddesses.

The idea of "goddess" as a symbol for all traits that are passive, creative, nurturing, and emotional is also a problematic one, which when applied to mythology does not bear out. As will be seen throughout the deck, there are countless goddesses who do not have any of these traits. It seems that regardless of the gender of a deity, they can have any trait known to humankind, whether it is creative or destructive, logical or emotional, peaceful or warlike, and it is this wonderful variety that we hope shines through in *Pistis Sophia: The Goddess Tarot*.

The Title

It took Nic and me around nine months to find a suitable name for this deck. We needed a title that would emphasize the academic approach we have taken to the goddesses contained in the cards, while also retaining the intuitive and spiritual aspect of working with this deck. It was our goal to reunite the intuitive, creative, spiritual approach with the logical, scholarly approach, with one informing the other.

I have long been interested in Gnostic texts from around the second century CE and was rereading some of them one day when I was reminded of the idea in many sects of what is now called Gnosticism—particularly the Valentinian tradition—that Wisdom and the Soul were embodied as feminine. In a text dating from sometime before the fourth century CE, found in the Nag Hammadi library in 1945, we read that "[w]ise men of old gave the soul a feminine name. Indeed she is female in her nature as well. She even has her womb" (Robinson 1990).

This text continues to use the imagery of the soul as a prostitute, giving herself to men in the hope that each new one that came along would be her true bridegroom and lead to her salvation. This allegory of the soul's journey as a veiled whore is one that is found repeatedly in literature about the feminine embodiment of Wisdom, and "the distinction between the street-walking whore looking for trade and the diligent wife seeking her husband is a fine one" (Matthews 2001, 95).

In the book of Proverbs, Wisdom is described as a woman crying aloud in the street, who later scolds those who do not attend to her quickly, and threatens to refuse them even though they search diligently for her:

> Out in the open wisdom calls aloud, she raises her voice in the public square; on top of the wall she cries out, at the city gate she makes her speech (Proverbs 1:20–21, New International Version [NIV]).

Throughout the Old Testament, New Testament, and Apocrypha, we find more references to Wisdom and the Soul as feminine beings (see Matthews 2001, 89–101). Yet one of the most beautiful pieces about her is found in the Nag Hammadi library, along with many other Gnostic texts, called *Thunder, Perfect Mind*. Spoken by what appears to be Wisdom herself in a series of paradoxical statements that mimic Greek identity riddles, we read about the nature of Wisdom and her femininity:

> I was sent forth from the power,
> and I have come to those who reflect upon me,
> and I have been found among those who seek after me.
> Look upon me, you who reflect upon me,
> and you hearers, hear me.
> You who are waiting for me, take me to yourselves.
> And do not banish me from your sight.
> And do not make your voice hate me, nor your hearing.
> Do not be ignorant of me anywhere or any time. Be on your guard!
> Do not be ignorant of me.
> For I am the first and the last.
> I am the honored one and the scorned one.
> I am the whore and the holy one.
> I am the wife and the virgin.
> I am ‹the mother› and the daughter.
> I am the members of my mother.
> I am the barren one
> and many are her sons (Robinson 1990).

The beginning of the text ("I was sent forth from the power") seems to reflect earlier Gnostic creation myths such as those found in *The Apocryphon of John*, wherein one of the first creations of the unnamed god was Forethought or Wisdom in female form. It continues with more paradoxical statements that point to the identity of the speaker as Wisdom.

This female Wisdom—not herself a goddess but instead an abstract concept given feminine form—seemed perfect for a goddess Tarot deck that lent itself to intellectual understanding and the intuitive use of these figures. So what is the name of this figure in the original language of many of these Gnostic texts? In Greek, *Sophia*. Further perusal of Gnostic texts revealed one called *Pistis Sophia*, which roughly translates to "faith–wisdom," indicating a close relationship and interplay in the spiritual realm between wisdom and intellectual understanding, and faith and intuitive understanding. Sophia herself was already cast as our High Priestess card. A one-card Tarot reading later, and we were sold on the name of the deck: we drew the High Priestess.

Structure of the Deck

It was our hope to create a deck that not only is useful to beginners but also provides more experienced readers with something different. As such, this deck displays a wide variety of inspiration from the Rider-Waite-Smith, the Crowley-Thoth, and the Marseilles standards. However, although these have provided us with the framework for the deck's structure, we have sought to make the images truly ours—we have not kept imagery or symbolism simply because it's been hallowed by decades of Tarot use. We have instead considered the meaning of each card and asked: Does it convey meaning to the reader? Does it express the nature of the goddess depicted? Does it allow for further research and study? Does it reveal too much, or is there room for the reader's own intuition to take over?

Thus, some card images may not be recognizable based on the traditional pictures associated with them. Our Sisters card (traditionally the Lovers), for instance, is not a romantic couple whose union is being blessed by an angel as it is in the Rider-Waite-Smith or the Crowley-Thoth. In fact, they are sisters sharing the recognition of their joint place of origin.

We have adhered to the traditional Tarot structure: we have 22 cards of the Major Arcana, 14 cards in each suit, and our own card meanings and associations do not often differ drastically from those traditionally assigned to the cards.

Mythology and the Tarot

As creators, Nic and I sought to unite two of our favorite subjects—Tarot and mythology. Both subjects speak so strongly to us that when we were creating the deck, not only did we come to understand more about the myths we were exploring, but we also added to our understanding of the concepts and archetypes represented in the Tarot.

Joseph Campbell said that myth has four functions: mystical, scientific, sociological, and psychological (Campbell 1988, 38–39). The mystical function of myth serves to reconcile consciousness to existence: The reality of life, in essence, is filled with suffering and pain, and when our consciousness perceives this, it has to either reconcile nature to existence or reject the monstrosity it perceives by saying it is something that should not have been. Myth enables us to reach a conclusion and justify it. Hence, the Gnostic myth of creation rejects the monstrous suffering in the world by attributing it to an idiotic demiurge as the creator of the world (Robinson 1990).

The scientific function of myth presents a single cosmological image of the universe and humankind's place within it that enables people to make sense of the mystery of life. Myths that tell a culture why living things die, why women menstruate, and how the Earth, sea, and sky interrelate or remain in their places serve this scientific function. However, in the modern world it would be easy to look down upon such myths, seeing science and technology as overriding them: After all, we now know for sure how the living body dies and decomposes, and can give scientific accounts of why this is necessary for the planet's ecosystem and balance. But while science and technology can explain to us the detailed mechanics of *how* it all works and occurs, they do not explain *why* it works. This is where myth still has a place.

The sociological function of myth is designed to validate and maintain the moral order by which a community or culture lives. Such myths may explain and encourage the community to refrain from eating certain foods; they may inform the community of what behavior is taboo and tell what happens if the taboo is broken; and they often include a revelatory element from a deity or culture hero giving a direct order about good and bad behavior. Thus, the God of the Old Testament delivered the Ten Commandments to Moses on Mount Sinai (Exodus 19–20), and Inuit stories tell of what happens to those who break the taboos of mourning and the dead (Rasmussen and Worster 1921, 110).

Finally, the psychological function of myth works to harmonize and deepen the psychological experiences of each individual as they go through life. It provides a model of the soul and how it progresses, as well as giving mundane events and occurrences (such as birth, adulthood, marriage, and aging) spiritual significance and meaning. A prime example of this function of myth can be seen in the Greek and Roman story of Eros and Psyche, or Cupid and Psyche, in which the soul (Psyche) experiences union, separation, and reunion with the divine and eventually becomes divine itself.

It is these four functions that we feel make mythology and Tarot close cousins. Just like myth, the Tarot can answer the "Why?" questions we so often ask when confronted with the reality of life; it can convey the values and social mores of the society we live in, and allow us to assess the value or morality of our actions and how they affect the wider community; it is also a powerful tool that enables us to understand our everyday lives and rites of passage in a meaningful and spiritual way. Whereas myths tell stories about the lives and acts of culture heroes and deities, the Tarot tells stories about our own lives. And just as mythology is a proactive, creative, living process created by storytellers who apply myths to listeners' lives, so the Tarot is always shifting and evolving, its stories and meaning being created by both the reader and the querent. In *The Power of Myth*, Bill Myers points out that "What human beings have in common is revealed by myths" (Campbell 1988, 4). This is also true of the Tarot, which—no matter where in the world it finds itself—retains a similar pattern and layout. The Tarot, along with myth, also bears the same themes and motifs that we find are universal to the human condition: concerns about birth, life, and death; the experience of love, transition, hope, need, community, anger, conflict and physical pain. If it wasn't for the language barrier among our wide range of countries and cultures, Tarot and mythology would provide us with an excellent way to bridge the gap and see just how much we all have in common.

Pistis Sophia: The Goddess Tarot is an unashamedly multicultural deck. This is not because we view all deities as one, but because we acknowledge the value of reading a wide variety of myths from different cultures. In doing so, we start to realize the universal and timeless themes of life and the human condition:

> Read myths. They teach you that you can turn inward, and you begin to get the message of the symbols. Read other people's myths, not those of your own religion, because you tend to interpret your own religion in terms of facts — but if you read the other ones, you begin to get the message (Campbell 1988, 5).

GETTING STARTED ON THE TAROT PATH

Studying Tarot can seem a daunting task at first. There seems to be so much to remember, so much to take in, so many avenues to explore, but that is part of the beauty of this area of discovery. Learning to use Tarot and gaining a deeper understanding of it is about getting lost in its journey, immersing yourself in its imagery, myths, and symbolism. The good news is that you already have the best foundation possible on which to build a relationship with the Tarot: You both speak the same language.

Tarot speaks in the language of symbolism. It is through imagery that its meanings are conveyed. We also speak and perceive in symbols, using them to navigate all aspects of our lives. The red color of a stop sign is symbolic; the logos of our well-loved brands are symbolic; the wearing of a wedding ring, or a nun's habit, or a medal of honor, is all symbolic. We are also raised to think symbolically: The media we grow up with, from news articles and movies to literature and fine art, rely on symbolism to trigger thought patterns, processes, and associations in our minds. Getting started on the Tarot path is simply a case of fine-tuning the language you've been speaking for years.

Approaches to learning Tarot can be categorized into two types: learning from others and learning from the self.

Learning from Others: Reading Tarot Publications

There are a great many books, magazine articles, web resources, and courses available to help you explore Tarot in its many different aspects. It can be tempting to view a single book as the sole truth about Tarot, but each book is only one person's perspective on the cards. Try to read widely, including both modern works and the classics by esoteric Tarot's earlier authors, such as Arthur Edward Waite and Aleister Crowley. When you've read a few different authors, you'll likely begin to see common threads running through their approaches and be able to identify what type of approach suits you best.

It is important to remember that no matter how much experience you gain with Tarot, another person's perspective on it always has the chance to expand your understanding further. Even if you are a professional reader with more than thirty years' experience, you will find that every now and then somebody publishes a work that revitalizes your own approach.

Learning from Others: Reading around the Subject

With many decks, including *Pistis Sophia: The Goddess Tarot*, the cards of the Tarot depict or draw on symbols, images, figures, scenes, and themes from other areas. This might be mythology, a certain culture, a certain style of artwork, a particular symbolic system, an aspect of life, or the work of a particular author or artist. It is useful to read around the subject of Tarot, exploring sources that inspired it or the work of more recent authors and artists. In particular, it can be fruitful to explore why an artist or author has associated a card with a certain myth, symbol, etc., since this can give you a greater understanding of the many possibilities of meaning and engagement. Remember—just because a book isn't explicitly about Tarot doesn't mean it is not relevant to your Tarot study.

Learning from the Self: Doing Readings

Studying Tarot is often a lot like self-directed study, since—unless you are undertaking a course run by somebody or an organization—you have only your own will and initiative to guide you. Learning from the self involves a lot of practical work—learning through doing.

One of the most important ways to learn Tarot from yourself is to do readings straight away. There is no moment at which you are "allowed" to start doing readings—you are ready the moment you pick up a Tarot pack for the first time (though you may not be very good!). Doing readings for yourself, friends, family, pets, and fictional characters allows you not only to develop your own approach but to gain an understanding of the card meanings in the context of a variety of situations, questions, and querents. You will also develop important reading skills naturally through doing readings, such as communication skills, interpretation skills, and how to link cards in a reading to each other and the question.

Learning from the Self: Invoking and Evoking Meaning

Symbols do not have a single fixed meaning; they both evoke and invoke meaning for each reader, so their focus may shift over time or change based on the reading, surrounding cards, inspiration, or influence from others. Exploring the cards' invoked and evoked meanings is a useful exercise and a way to rejuvenate your understanding of certain cards if it feels like it has become stagnant.

> When a card **invokes** meaning, it draws on traditional symbolic understanding that is often found in culture, symbolic systems, religion, or history.
>
> When a card **evokes** meaning, it pulls out of the individual a personal response

to the symbol on the basis of experience, understanding, aesthetics, feeling, and moment.

For example, the invoked meanings of a lion include the astrological sign of Leo, the alchemical symbol of unrefined matter, the alchemical symbol of sulfur, and the Kabbalistic symbol of the sephira of Geburah. The evoked meanings of the same symbol will be different for each person and each reading but could include the lion being the querent's power animal, the querent's son being named Leo, a link to the literary figure of Aslan from C. S. Lewis's *Chronicles of Narnia,* and what the figure means to the querent, etc.

A Tarot reader can discover both the invoked and evoked meanings of a symbol and therefore a Tarot card and recognizes both as equally important. Books on Tarot and symbolism can often tell you some of the invoked meanings of various symbols that traditionally appear in the cards, but one of your tasks as a reader is to discover new ways in which a symbol presents itself, new dimensions of meaning. In doing so, you will eventually build up your own inner mindscape for each card and deepen your understanding of the card meanings.

Learning from the Self: Keeping a Tarot Journal

Some Tarot readers keep a Tarot journal in which they record all their thoughts, realizations, readings, and more. The ways in which a Tarot journal is kept are as varied as the reader—one of the joys of it is making it your own. Some people enjoy hand writing their journal in a notebook; others prefer keeping a ring binder to which they can add sheets as they write them and reorder them; some like to scrapbook their journal; others prefer typing on a computer.

You can include anything you like in your journal, but just a few suggestions include:

- records of your readings
- diary entries of your insights
- helpful quotes from books
- sketches/collages of cards
- spreads you find useful
- daily draw entries (see below)
- things you'd like to research
- exercises with the cards
- notes from books you are reading
- notes from Tarot workshops you attend
- reading lists of books you want

- list of decks you'd like to buy
- poetry or other creative writing on the cards
- information about symbolism

The Tarot journal is most useful for making the Tarot journey your own. It helps you learn in the way you learn best, tailoring your Tarot path to suit your needs.

Learning from the Self: Daily Draw

Tarot most fully integrates into the psyche when it is practiced or engaged with regularly. Having a regular practice of drawing a card or performing a short reading not only deepens your understanding of the cards but also improves your reading technique and develops your Tarot voice.

For a daily draw, pick one card at random from your deck, either in the morning or evening. If you do this in the morning, spend a few minutes examining the card and asking yourself what it might foretell for the coming day. What awaits you? What strength will you need? What challenges might you face? What will be the theme of the day? If you do it in the evening, spend some time reflecting on what has happened and how the card relates to it. It is most useful to write a paragraph or two about your reflections in your Tarot journal or to give yourself a reading stating these reflections aloud. Doing this encourages you to put into coherent form what might otherwise remain unformed and half interpreted.

If a daily draw is too frequent for you, you could try a weekly draw. If you do, try drawing three cards instead. An important aspect of this practice is to see how the cards relate to real life in terms that you are familiar with.

Learning from the Self: Symbolic Study of the Cards

A good way to learn about the cards beyond simply reading what somebody else has written about them is to deeply study them. This can be done systematically, working through the cards in order, or as part of a daily/weekly journaling exercise or daily/weekly random card draw.

When you have chosen/drawn a card to study, ask yourself what symbols it contains. These can include colors, animals, activity, mood, atmosphere, objects, nature, the age of people, the gender of people, weather, and natural occurrences. Allow the symbolism to come alive in your mind so that it can stimulate your knowledge and intuition. A Tarot card might say something different to you each time you look at it, so try to remove all preconceptions when you examine it. Some useful ways of approaching a card include the following:

- What are your initial feelings about the card?
- What do these symbols mean to you (evoke)?
- Is there a theme in these symbols?
- What are your feelings about the card now that you have examined the symbolism?
- What symbols stand out for you?
- How do these symbols relate to each other?
- What do books say about the card meaning?
- How does this card relate to various symbolic systems (invoke meaning)?

Learning from the Self: The Three-Symbol Reading

The three-symbol reading is a useful exercise for when you feel your intuition or ideas about card meanings are becoming stagnant. Simply draw a single card and examine it, then pick three symbols that stand out to you from the card image: one from the foreground, one from the midground, and one from the background. Don't think too hard about them, and try to allow the symbols you choose to be those that you see first or that stand out.

Each of these symbols expresses a meaning in a different context:

The symbol in the **foreground** tells you about what has the greatest influence on you at this time, or brings out an issue that is on your mind.

The symbol in the **midground** tells you about influences, events, or circumstances that are acting on you but aren't as clear to you or as obvious.

The symbol in the **background** tells you what is hidden or unexpected, or what you are unaware of that has an influence on you at the time.

This exercise gives you a quick, simple reading and helps you improve your ability to link symbols and cards.

READING WITH
PISTIS SOPHIA: THE GODDESS TAROT

One of the most common uses of the Tarot pack is for divination—performing readings with the cards to gain answers to questions. The process of Tarot reading can also be used to solve problems, to brainstorm an idea or project, to grant inspiration for creative writing, or as a form of self-therapy.

Although it has often been shrouded in mysticism, the process of performing a Tarot reading is very simple. It consists of four steps, around which you may pack other steps, performances, or habits:

1. Deciding on the question, issue, situation, or subject
2. Randomizing the cards
3. Drawing the cards and laying them out
4. Interpreting the cards

Randomizing the cards can involve any manner of shuffling, swirling on a table, choosing cards from a fan, or perhaps even throwing them on the floor. The way you randomize your cards will depend on your personal preference and the type of reading you are performing. A sit-down reading with a querent may require a simpler shuffling of the deck; it may also be suitable for the querent to choose the cards for the reading from the fanned-out deck.

Laying out the cards in a spread is optional. Interpreting the cards, generally, requires them to be visible, so they should be placed in front of you / the querent; however, the pattern (spread) in which they are laid is dependent on your preferences, the type of reading, and the querent. It is acceptable to simply lay them down side by side as you draw them. It is also acceptable if you want to use a complicated pattern for your reading and interpret not only the cards but where they land in that pattern. You may find, especially if you are new to Tarot interpretation, that it is easier to use a small spread, since the spread's positions will guide you in interpreting the cards and provide you with a framework for the reading. It is also fine to move cards around the table to highlight similarities, differences, connections, and more—try experimenting with different styles to see what you prefer and which are more suited to certain types of question and querent.

Interpreting the cards is a process that varies greatly from reader to reader. Often, it is a process that occurs without us noticing it, since our minds naturally think in symbols and are trained from an early age to interpret the meanings conveyed by images. When interpreting a reading, you are thinking about the meanings of both the individual cards and the reading as a whole—how the cards connect, influence each other, and support each other. While you could just read a traditional card meaning from a book to interpret a reading, you will find that the position of a card in the spread, the question asked, the situation being discussed, the other cards in the spread, and intuition/inspiration will direct the more general card meaning toward something specific; it might even alter from its traditional meaning.

Some aspects you might take into consideration when interpreting an individual card and the whole reading are

- the traditional card meanings
- the position of each card and what that adds to the traditional meaning
- color symbolism. Is one color particularly dominant in the spread, for example?
- numerological symbolism. Does one number appear more frequently than others among the cards? Is there a lack of certain numbers?
- elemental symbolism. If a reading is heavy on Air cards, as well as on symbols of air, what could this mean? This might suggest the area of life that the reading is most concerned with, or point to an overwhelming influence of a particular feeling, behavior, or concern. Imbalances of an element can also be telling: No water symbolism in a relationship reading? Consider what the lack of something suggests.

At first you might find you need to examine these things systematically, but eventually you will find that you start to see them automatically. You should allow both traditional understandings of the cards and intuitive responses to them to inform your interpretations. The pages in this guidebook that examine each card explore various aspects of the card meanings and highlight possible ways of applying them to a reading, but they are not the only possible ways to interpret the cards.

XVII THE STAR
Ushas

XVIII THE MOON
Morgan la Fey

PISTIS SOPHIA: THE GODDESS TAROT

There are innumerable Tarot spreads that can be used for readings. They can be found in books about Tarot and online, or they can be created by you. Some are more traditional and well known, whereas others may never be used by anyone other than their creator. Here you will find some spreads created for use with *Pistis Sophia: The Goddess Tarot*, inspired by goddesses both featured in the deck and not, and their myths, symbols, or themes.

"Brigid of the Mantles" Spread
A SPREAD ABOUT CREATIVITY

Brigid, the Irish goddess and saint mentioned from the seventh century CE onward, is identified as the patron of poetry, creativity, smithwork, cattle, and healing. This spread examines our own creativity, using a verse from a hymn to St. Brigid from the *Carmina Gadelica*—each line giving us a card position in the spread.

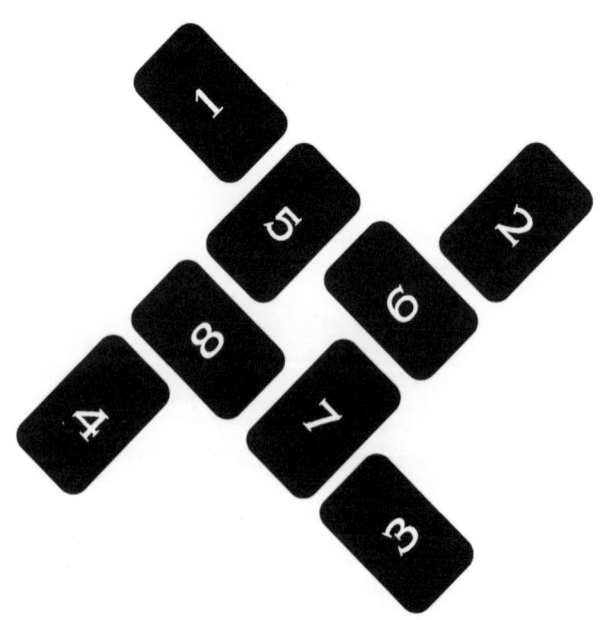

Brigit of the mantles,
Brigit of the peat-heap,
Brigit of the twining hair,
Brigit of the augury.
Brigit of the white feet,
Brigit of the calmness,
Brigit of the white palms,
Brigit of the kine.
(*Carmina Gadelica* 263, trans. in Carmichael 1940, 157)

CARD 1: The patron of your inspiration
CARD 2: The fuel for your inspiration
CARD 3: The way your inspiration manifests in the external world
CARD 4: Where your inspiration will take you next
CARD 5: How you put your creativity to work
CARD 6: What natural talents you have that contribute to your creativity
CARD 7: How you are guided during your creative process
CARD 8: How your inspiration and creativity affect your community and others around you.

"Descent to the Heaven Below" Spread
A SPREAD ABOUT TRANSFORMATION

This spread is based on the Rebirth card, and the accompanying myth of Inanna's descent into the Netherworld (called "Heaven Below" or the "Great Below"), and her death in the darkness there at the hands of her elder sister Ereškigal, Queen of the Netherworld. Inanna rots in the Netherworld for three days and nights before being reborn into the Great Above once more, and her descent into the Netherworld is seen as a mythological expression of our own spiritual descent. As she descends, she is stopped at each of seven gates and stripped of one of her seven items of power, so that she enters her sister's throne room completely naked and bowed low, ready to undergo death and rebirth.

The Descent to the Heaven Below spread is one that can be used to discover what it is you must first strip away from your life before you can begin a process of transformation. It can be used at any turning point in your life where you feel a transition process is beginning, and where you feel it may be blocked by obstacles.

(The quotes from the myth used here are those found in Wolkstein and Kramer 1983.)

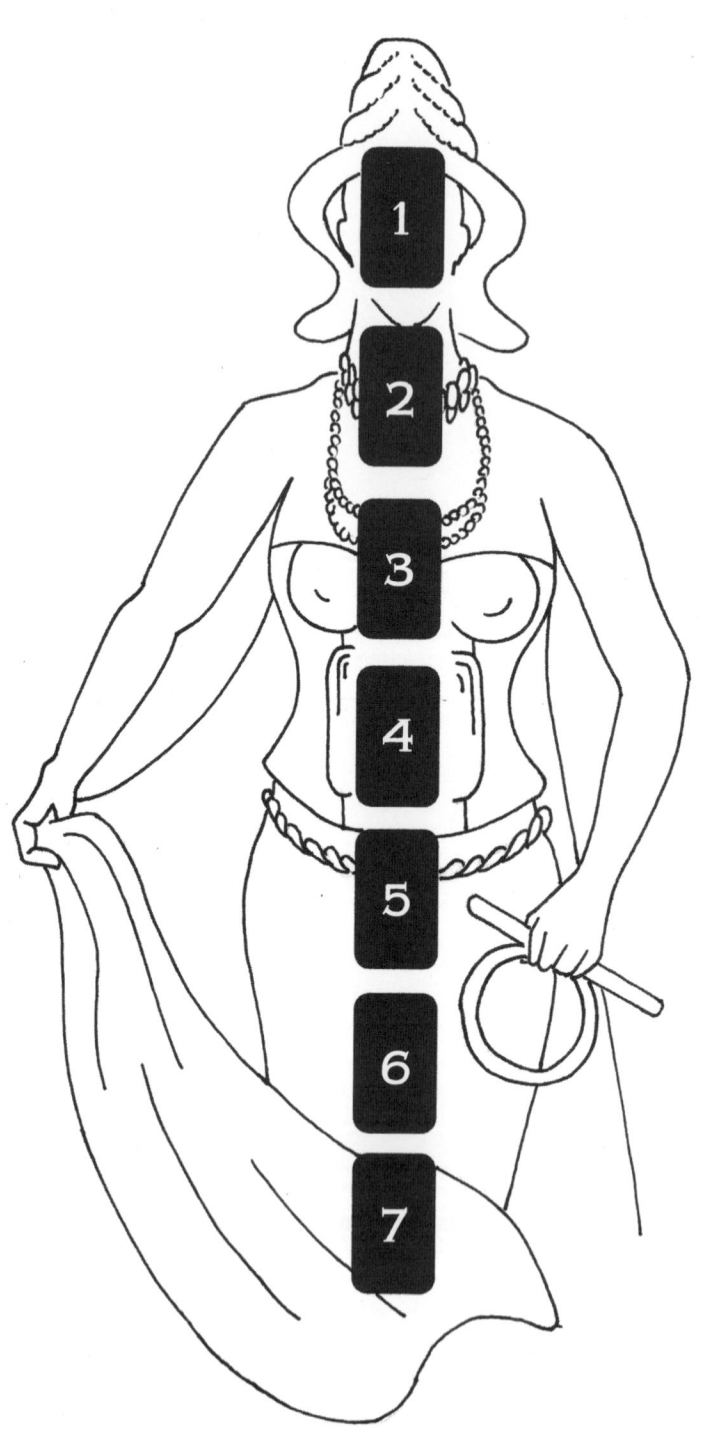

CARD 1: *"When she entered the first gate, from her head, the shugurra, the crown of the steppe, was removed."*

That which feeds your ego.

CARD 2: *"When she entered the second gate, from her neck the small lapis beads were removed."*

The persona you show to the world around you.

CARD 3: *"When she entered the third gate, from her breast the double strand of beads was removed."*

That which holds back your heart.

CARD 4: *"When she entered the fourth gate, from her chest the breastplate called 'Come, man, come!' was removed."*

The barriers you put up between yourself and others as protection.

CARD 5: *"When she entered the fifth gate, from her waist the gold ring was removed."*

That which distracts you.

CARD 6: *"When she entered the sixth gate, from her hand the lapis measuring rod and line was removed."*

The way you judge and measure others.

CARD 7: *"When she entered the seventh gate, from her body the royal robe was removed."*

That which you fear the loss of most.

"Naked and bowed low, Inanna entered the throne room."

If you wish to undertake further examination of this, you can draw a second card for each position, detailing how you can begin to strip away each obstacle and drawback revealed by the first set of cards.

"Flowers of Blodeuwedd" Spread

A SPREAD ABOUT OUTWARD APPEARANCES

The Welsh figure Blodeuwedd, found in the *Mabinogion*, was a woman created from flowers by the magician Gwydion. The *Mabinogion* has her made from the flowers of oak, broom, and meadowsweet. Her myth tells how this beautiful creature—so lovely to look at, and a fitting wife for the hero Llew Llaw Gyffes—betrayed her husband so that she could be with another man. Her outward appearance—that of the doting wife and mistress of the household—hid her inner feelings.

Flowers have been used for centuries in the English-speaking world to denote a wide variety of things—we all know that red roses signify passionate love, and many people associate daisies with innocence and childhood, or bluebells with whimsy. In Victorian England, an entire language of flowers was developed: thus, a single blossom delivered to an admirer could very quickly rebuff unwanted attention or confirm mutual feelings. An entire bouquet, carefully arranged, could create a "document," a larger and more detailed sentiment.

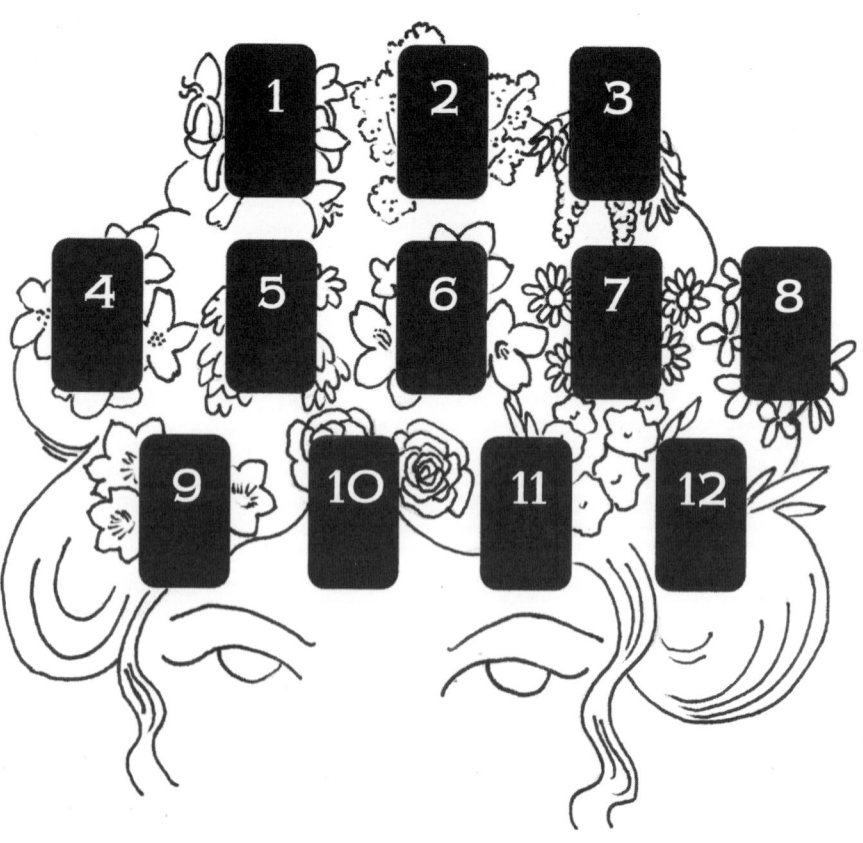

This Tarot spread is about your outward appearances to others and the world—the masks you wear and how you act. The card positions have been chosen based on Victorian messages associated with each type of flower.

CARD 1: Broom—*Devotion*—*"I am ever yours."*

How do you show people that you are willing to give them your time and energy?

CARD 2: Meadowsweet—*Uselessness*—*"I look for a lover who is something more than merely decorative."*

When you feel lost or unable to achieve a goal, how do you act and what face do you show to the world?

CARD 3: Oak—*Courage*—*"Do not despair; love will find a way."*

How do you outwardly express courage and strength?

CARD 4: Apple Blossom—*Beauty and goodness*—*"You are as good as you are beautiful."*

How do you attract people to yourself?

CARD 5: Bracken—*Enchantment*—*"You fascinate me."*

What do you need people to believe about you?

CARD 6: Cherry Blossom—*Increase*—*"To the ripening of our friendship!"*

How do you demonstrate your friendship?

CARD 7: Feverfew—*Protection*—*"Let me shield you."*

What actions do you take to protect those around you?

CARD 8: Gilliflower—*Affection*—*"You are very dear to me."*

How do you relate to people in public? How do you show affection outwardly?

CARD 9: Hellebore—*Lying tongues*—*"Do not believe any ill tales of me. I can explain everything."*

When you need to communicate something to others, what attitude do you convey?

CARD 10: Red Rose—*Love*—*"I love you."*

When you are in love, what face do you present to the world?

CARD 11: Gladiolus—*Pain*—*"Your words have wounded me."*

When you are hurt, what face do you show to the world?

CARD 12: The Bouquet—As an overall picture, what kind of person does the world see in you?

The "Goddess Archetype" Spread
A SPREAD TO EXPLORE THE SELF

CARD 1: **Mother**—What do you nurture? How do you create?

CARD 2: **Virgin**—What is a mystery to you? How do you celebrate your image?

CARD 3: **Siren**—What attracts others to you? How can you celebrate your sexuality?

CARD 4: **Sorceress**—What do you control and manipulate? How can you change your life?

CARD 5: **Wisewoman**—What do you know deeply? How can you share your knowledge?

CARD 6: **Fairy Godmother**—What gifts can you give to the world and others? How do others approach you?

CARD 7: **Wife**—What are you married to? How do you devote yourself to things?

CARD 8: **Hag**—What in you is ugly and terrifying? How can you redeem this monster?

CARD 9: **Amazon**—What would you fight for? How can you develop your courage and determination?

"Handmaidens of Sophia" Spread

A SPREAD ABOUT ASSESSING AND ACCESSING OUR KNOWLEDGE

Sophia, the embodied form of wisdom found in our High Priestess card, is said to have had seven handmaidens or daughters, each of whom ruled over a type of knowledge or intellectual pursuit. In the Middle Ages, each of these handmaidens was also associated with one of the seven classical planets.

This spread examines our relationship with our own knowledge and highlights ways we can access it or make better use of it.

CARD 1: **Grammar**—*Moon*—How you express your learning and knowledge.

CARD 2: **Rhetoric**—*Venus*—How you examine subjects and approach learning.

CARD 3: **Dialectic**—*Mercury*—How you respond to the knowledge of others.

CARD 4: **Arithmetic**—*Mars*—How your knowledge is put to use in your everyday life.

CARD 5: **Geometry**—*Jupiter*—How you gauge your level of knowledge and accomplishment.

CARD 6: **Music**—*Sun*—How your knowledge improves you as a person, and the understanding it leads to.

CARD 7: **Astronomy**—*Saturn*—Where your knowledge will lead you.

"Seven Stabs of the Knife" Spread

A SPREAD TO EXAMINE AND HEAL WOUNDS, HURT, BETRAYAL, AND CONFLICT

Seven stabs of the knife,

Seven stabs of the sword.

The day my blood runs down

I will vomit my blood and give it to them.

Erzulie Dantor is the Vodou spirit who protects the oppressed and injured. In her legend she was stabbed seven times by those she thought were her comrades in the Haitian Revolution. Yet her unstoppable strength and persistence remained, and she guides those who feel wronged, protects those who are hurt by others, and helps us respond to pain and conflict.

Each position in this spread recalls one of the sword wounds inflicted upon Erzulie Dantor, and in the Catholic imagery that was syncretized with Vodou, these are also the seven sorrows of Mary, Mother of Christ.

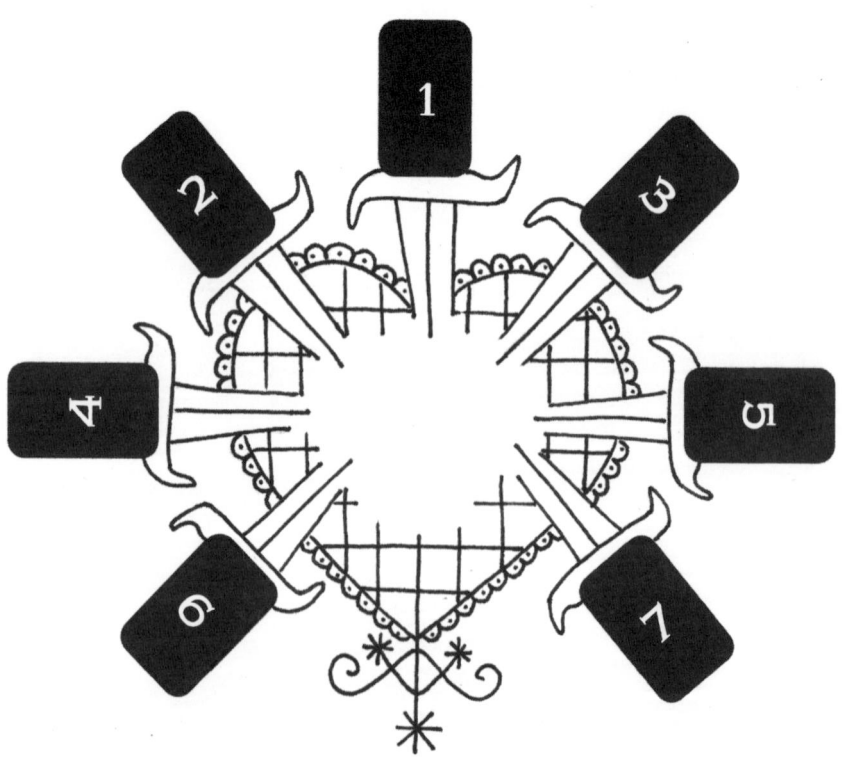

CARD 1: What is the foundation or root of this hurt/conflict?

CARD 2: Is the hurt related to or caused by another person, or yourself? How so?

CARD 3: How are you currently responding to the hurt or conflict on an external level?

CARD 4: How are you currently responding to the hurt or conflict on an internal level?

CARD 5: What is the first step of the healing process? What do you need to learn or acknowledge to facilitate growth?

CARD 6: What effect might this hurt or conflict have on you in the future?

CARD 7: What is your greatest strength in responding positively to, and surviving, hurt, pain, and conflict?

CARD MEANINGS

The Major Arcana are the cards that people most often imagine when Tarot is mentioned. With their evocative images and timeless subjects, it is these cards that are usually found in movies, works of art, and other media. As their name suggests, the 22 cards of the Major Arcana offer us symbolic representations of important aspects of the universe and of human life: love, death, temptation, destruction, change, manifestation, authority, balance, and more. They are conversely the most abstract cards, since the concepts they depict are so vast, and the cards that we are closest to as human beings, for they are universal concepts that represent truths of life.

The symbols of the Major Arcana can be interpreted systematically. Numerology, astrology, and color symbolism all contribute to the meanings of these cards. A wider study of astrology in relation to all the cards of the Tarot is not necessary for interpretation but will greatly enhance your understanding of the cards and their more traditional representations. For this deck, which does not rely on astrological symbolism, it is enough to know the traditional associations of the classical planets and zodiac signs to the Major Arcana cards. Each of these cards also has a Kabbalistic letter associated with them, which can be studied to gain greater understanding of some of the aspects of meaning.

MAJOR ARCANA	ASTROLOGICAL ASSOCIATION	KABBALISTIC ASSOCIATION
The Fool	Uranus	Aleph
The Magician	Mercury	Beth
The High Priestess	Moon	Gimel
The Empress	Venus	Daleth
The Construct (The Emperor)	Aries	Heh
The Hierophant	Taurus	Vav
The Sisters (The Lovers)	Gemini	Zayin
The Chariot	Cancer	Cheth
Strength	Leo	Teth
The Hermit	Virgo	Yod
The Wheel of Fortune	Jupiter	Kaph
Justice	Libra	Lamed
The Mystic (The Hanged Man)	Neptune	Mem
Death	Scorpio	Nun
Alchemy (Temperance)	Sagittarius	Samekh
The Devil	Capricorn	Ayin
The Tower	Mars	Peh
The Star	Aquarius	Tzaddi
The Moon	Pisces	Qoph
The Sun	Sun	Resh
Rebirth	Pluto	Shin
The Universe	Saturn	Tav

0 THE FOOL

Eve
BIBLICAL

Beneath the clear blue skies of the Garden of Eden, Eve, naked and innocent and unashamed, stretches her hand out to grasp the fruit from the Tree of Knowledge of Good and Evil. A snake looks on, coiled around her shoulder, its tongue flicking out to taste the air and urge her onward. Eve longs to discover truth, and she wishes to share the knowledge of God with her husband, Adam, and thus she takes the risk on the advice of a lower creature and takes the first step toward Life.

As above . . .

GODDESSES AND SYMBOLS

The story of Eve is well known to many people around the world, since it is found in the Christian and Jewish religions as well as in Islam. Her name in Arabic is Hawwa, although she is not referred to by name in the Qu'ran and instead is called Adam's wife. The Arabic and Hebrew versions of her name both mean, variously, "source of life," "bringer of life," and "life." In later Greek translations of the Hebrew Bible, her name is transliterated as Heua (with the "u" being pronounced much later as a "v"), and in some versions, such as the Septuagint (an ancient Greek translation), the name is given as Zoe, meaning "life." This name seems appropriate for a woman who, according to *The Life of Adam and Eve*, a collection of texts dating from around the first century BCE, birthed thirty sons and thirty daughters. According to the Bible, Eve was created by God from one of Adam's ribs, giving to Adam a helper and mate:

"Then the Lord God made a woman from the rib he had taken out of the man, and he brought her to the man. The man said, 'This is now bone of my bones and flesh of my flesh; she shall be called "woman," for she was taken out of man.' For this reason a man will leave his father and mother and be united to his wife, and they will become one flesh. The man and his wife were both naked, and they felt no shame" (Genesis 2:20–25, New International Version).

Many interpreters down through the ages have used this as a reason to give women fewer rights than men, stating that women are to serve men and be subordinate to them, just as Eve was created as a helper for Adam. However, Eve became the main protagonist in the biblical story of human origin, since it was she who yearned to gain the wisdom that had been withheld from both her and Adam since God made them. On the advice of a crafty serpent, who assured her that she would not die upon eating the Fruit of the Tree of Knowledge of Good and Evil, Eve ate the fruit:

> You will not surely die, the serpent said to the woman. For God knows that when you eat of it, your eyes will be opened, and you will be like God, knowing good and evil. When the woman saw that the fruit of the tree was good for food and pleasing to the eye, and also desirable for gaining wisdom, she took some and ate it. She also gave some to her husband, who was with her, and he ate it. Then the eyes of both of them were opened, and they realized that they were naked; so they sewed fig leaves together and made coverings for themselves (Genesis 3:4–7, NIV).

Eve's action not only gained wisdom for herself but also for her husband, and because of this action she became the mother of humanity. The act, conceived in ignorance and blissful nonawareness, sparked a chain of events that led to the whole of human experience. Although God "cursed" Adam and Eve with suffering, toil, pain in childbirth, and death, Eve also won the gift of being able to create life and experience the things that would bring her wisdom. The state of man and woman in the Garden of Eden can be viewed as a childlike state of ignorance, and through the "Fall" they found themselves thrown into life. Eve is therefore not only the mother of the human race through her actions but, in a sense, is also mother of Adam. This view was held by Phyllis Trible, who viewed Eve as the crown and pinnacle of creation, independent in her actions, while Adam was passive yet written as the more powerful partner in the relationship (Trible 1973). Eve's actions may have been foolish, but that is to be expected when she did not have wisdom, knowledge, or experience to inform her actions.

After Eve ate the fruit and shared it with her husband, both were expelled from the Garden of Eden:

> And the Lord God said, "The man has now become like one of us, knowing good and evil. He must not be allowed to reach out his hand and take also from the tree of life and eat, and live for ever (Genesis 3:22, NIV).

It is interesting to note here that God acknowledged that by her action, Eve made herself and Adam like him; the specific knowledge gained is also defined as the knowledge of good and evil—an understanding gained by children as they grow up, but not automatically given to infants at birth. Therefore, Eve raised herself and Adam from a state of infancy to one of moral awareness. Barbara Smith put this dynamic well while discussing Pandora (with whom Eve is frequently compared):

> Like the Judaeo-Christian myth of Eve, the currency of man's fall is women's wish for knowledge (Larrington 1992, 95).

Despite this, early Christian writers did not view Eve in a positive way, instead granting her various epithets such as "road of iniquity," "daughter of falsehood," "sentinel of Hell," and "enemy of peace." They gave to her the most part in original sin, and by association, all women were given this blame. Later writers, including the authors of the *Malleus Maleficarum* ("The Hammer of the Witches"), used Eve's "betrayal" as justification for direct discrimination against women, and a late-sixteenth-century scholar, Valentius Acidalius, wrote a pamphlet titled "Women do not have a soul and do not belong to the human race, as is shown by many passages of Holy Scripture." However, Gnostic Christianity gave Eve a more elevated role, equating her with Sophia as Light-Maiden; as "Zoe" she was also seen as a daughter of Sophia, and therefore part of the supreme feminine principle.

In contrast to most medieval views of Eve, a song (in Middle English) dating from the fifteenth century offers a more positive representation. It describes Adam chained up for 4,000 years as punishment for taking the fruit (in this song, an apple) of the Tree of Knowledge, and goes on to say that the act of eating this fruit was the very act that brought about the redemption of mankind and the birth of the Virgin Mary (Blessed Queen of Heaven) and thereby Jesus Christ. Therefore, the song concludes, we should praise God and thank him for the act. Although the song does not mention Eve, it was Eve who took the fruit and so it is her act that brought about redemption, Mary, and her son.

Adam lay ybounden,

Bounden in a bond;

Four thousand winters,

Thought he not too long.

And all was for an apple,

An apple that he took.

As clerkes finden,

Written in their book.

Ne had the apple taken been,

The apple taken been,

Ne had never our ladie,

Abeen heav'ne queen.

Blessed be the time

That apple taken was,

Therefore we moun singen.

Deo gracias! (Wright 1856, 32–33)

It is interesting that many centuries of commentary on Eve have given her the role of temptress, beguiler, and disingenuous helper of Satan, giving wicked counsel to Adam and forcing him—with her wicked ways, often sexually—to eat the fruit. These comments usually compare Eve to the serpent, juxtaposing the serpent's temptation of Eve with Eve's temptation of Adam. Yet the biblical text simply reads "she also gave some to her husband, who was with her." There is no temptation or wicked counsel reported in the original text. This giving of the apple, if it is indeed temptation, puts God in the role of original tempter, as Jean Higgins writes:

> According to such logic, God too would be tempter and cause of sin, for God "gave" Adam his wife; and God "gave" Adam the garden to keep, with the forbidden tree in the middle of it. God also created the serpent (Higgins 1976, 642).

It's almost as if the Fall was intended to happen from the beginning.

. . . So below

DIVINATORY MEANINGS

In a reading, the Fool is a card of new beginnings and fresh opportunities, which often bring with them some risk, either in the initial choice to take them or in the consequences thereof. It is also a card of great paradox, since it contains both the concept of ignorance and foolishness as well as a state of purity, blessedness, sanctity, and wisdom. It brings with it change, but not the kind of destructive or decaying change you might find indicated by Death or the Tower cards; rather, this is a movement forward into a new stage. It is not the transition period, however, but the new opportunity itself.

Sometimes this card can appear in a reading as a warning to the querent that their actions are foolish and may produce undesirable results—there is always a pitfall awaiting the fool that rushes in where angels fear to tread. Yet, at other times it can advise the querent to take the opportunities they are being given, regardless of the risks that might be involved—nothing ventured, nothing gained! Often, it indicates that the querent is on a path where they are not thinking very far ahead, not making plans, just enjoying the journey itself, taking every day as it comes. This is the lust for life, the living for living's sake.

The Fool also reminds us that if we do not take the first step, we can never begin our journey. It can indicate that the road in front of the querent will be long and take them to places entirely unexpected; it says that the querent is the Fool, inexperienced in this area and uncertain, yet they should start the journey anyway. In their innocence or inexperience is the blessing of beginner's mind, the joy of something new, the fresh perspective they will need to get them through. In the face of jaded cynicism, the Fool brings with it a charming laughter that pities those too experienced to enjoy life anymore.

This card can also suggest somebody (perhaps the querent, or somebody else in their life) who finds it hard to settle down, or who seems to be playing the fool. This person is a wanderer, always looking to the next horizon, the eternal student always looking to discover more. They understand that in comparison to the vast expanse of the universe, they know nothing. This can make them seem, to others, unreliable and immature. But sometimes that is what is needed to shake things up.

KEYWORDS

New beginnings; freshness; opportunity; journey; curiosity; risk; joy; optimism; hope; carefree, childlike, childish; purity; naivety; innocence; free spirit; independence; foolishness; ignorance

I THE MAGICIAN

Isis
EGYPTIAN

As pure white light refracts into a spectrum of color and the planets begin to move into their cosmic positions, the great mother goddess Isis pulls the energy of the gods down into manifestation; this act of creation is an act of magic and will. From the eye of Ra, from whom she stole the secrets of magic, Isis has control of the four elements and thus the entirety of the world. Beneath her is the knot of Isis (the *tyet*), an Egyptian symbol representing life, vitality, and power, particularly the breath of life. As Isis creates and controls using her magic, she places herself at the center of the universe.

As above . . .

GODDESSES AND SYMBOLS

His sister was his guard,

She who drives off the foes,

Who stops the deeds of the disturber

By the power of her utterance.

The clever-tongued whose speech fails not,

Effective in the word of command,

Mighty Isis who protected her brother,

Who sought him without wearying.

Who roamed the land lamenting him,

Who made a shade with her plumage,

Created breath with her wings.

Who jubilated, joined her brother,

Raised the weary one's inertness,

Received the seed, bore the heir,

Raised the child in solitude,

His abode unknown.

Who brought him when his arm was strong

Into the broad hall of Geb (The Great Hymn to Osiris on the stele of Amenmose, Eighteenth Dynasty; Lichtheim 2006b, 83–84).

Isis is called by many names and epithets, especially in the Egyptian *Book of the Dead*. These include "She Who Gives Birth to Heaven and Earth," "Great Lady of Magic," "Mistress of the House of Life," "Lady of the Words of Power," "Light-Giver of Heaven," "The One Who Is All," and "Star of the Sea" (Williams 1985, 109–19). The standard epithet for Isis was *weret hekau*—great of magic. Egyptian mythology is filled with examples of Isis's magical ability, her cunning and guile, her mastery of the world of the gods and of humans, her role as mother of Horus and the Pharaohs, and her identity as sister-wife of Osiris.

As with most ancient deities, the origin of Isis's worship is difficult to establish, but we know that her most important sanctuary was at Behbeit El-Hagar in the Nile delta, and that she had temples, sanctuaries, and shrines all over the Mediterranean world. Her cult was strongly established by the time of predynastic Egypt (prior to 3,200 BCE) and continued well into the Christian era in the Roman world, in the form of the *Navigium Isidis* ("the vessel of Isis"), a Roman festival for the goddess held yearly and still recorded in the fourth century CE (Alföldi 1938, 88–90). There is even suggestion that her worship spread as far as the British Isles—an inscription on an earthenware jug found in Southwark, dating from the second century CE, mentions a temple to Isis in London that first fell into disrepair but was later refurbished.

Isis's name was more likely to have been Aset or Usat (ancient Egyptian hieroglyphs do not have vowels, so the name "Isis" is simply a convenient convention) and translates as "throne." Her headdress is usually depicted as a throne, and the hieroglyph of her name features a throne. In this aspect, Isis was seen as the mother and the seat of power of the pharaoh (in the New Kingdom period, she was often depicted nursing the pharaoh, and Thutmose III was depicted in his tomb as suckling from a sycamore tree—also a symbol of Isis—that had a breast), who himself took on the role of Horus, the son of Osiris, ruler of Egypt, who overcame the forces of Set (who represented chaos and evil). As such, Isis was the source of a ruler's power, the originator and channel of it. Her name appears over eighty times in the *Pyramid Texts*, a series of funerary texts, in which she is depicted as aiding the dead pharaoh as he passed to the next stage. She was also called the mother of the "four sons of Horus," these being the four canopic jars that contained the essential organs of the deceased pharaoh.

It is clear that as time went on, Isis subsumed other goddesses into herself, and her cult and aspects of her worship took on features from these other Goddess cults. As such, later depictions of Isis show her with the solar disk and horns of the mother goddess Hathor (as she is also shown in the card image), and in this role as mother she has one of the most important roles of the Osirian myth cycle. This cycle is told to us most coherently by Plutarch in his treatise *De Iside et Osiride*, and though he was not Egyptian himself, it is understood that he was retelling a well-known Egyptian myth from the time. The story tells us that Isis was the daughter of Nut and Geb, sister of Osiris, Set, and Nephthys. She was given to Osiris as his wife (it is interesting to note that Osiris's name was likely to have been closer to Usir, also meaning "throne," linking both him and his sister-wife to the seat of power of the pharaoh). Set was jealous of their happiness and wanted to kill his brother so that he might rule over Egypt instead, so he had craftsmen make a coffin to Osiris's exact measurements, and held a party. During this, he presented the beautifully crafted coffin and said that whoever it fit best could have it. Each guest took turns trying it, but nobody fit; when Osiris lay down in it, he found that it fit, but Set's servants slammed the lid shut and hammered nails in before anybody could stop them, and threw Osiris in his coffin into the river. Osiris drowned, and when Isis heard of her husband's death, she wept bitterly and searched for his body. However, Set knew that his sister was skilled in the ways of magic and would revive her husband if she found his body, so he found it first and dismembered it, scattering it in fourteen pieces across the land of Egypt. Isis refused to end her search, and she eventually gathered together all the pieces (though in some accounts the fourteenth piece, Osiris's phallus, was missing, so she replaced it with a phallus of gold) and breathed just enough life back into Osiris's body to conceive a son, Horus.

This story highlights Isis's skill at magic and the power she has to breathe life into the nonliving. She owns power and can give it and restore it. The method by which she obtained this magical power, however, is told in a story from the *Turin Papyrus of the Nineteenth Dynasty* (1320–1205 BCE), which shows the cunning of Isis:

> Now Isis was a clever woman. Her heart was craftier than a million men; she was choicier than a million gods; she was more discerning than a million of the noble dead. There was nothing that she did not know in heaven and Earth, like Re, who made the content of the Earth. The goddess purposed in her heart to learn the name of the august god (Pritchard 1969, 12).

The true name of Ra was his power; in ancient Egypt, the name was the source of any individual's power and soul. Ra, knowing this, had dozens of different names but did not reveal to anybody his true name, knowing it would give them power over him. Isis, however, was clever. She made a poisonous serpent to bite Ra and fill him with its venom, and as he lay dying from the poison she told him that she could heal him, but only if he first gave her his power—his true name. Seeing no other option, Ra gave her his name, and Isis gained the knowledge and skill of magic. The magic of the name is inextricably linked with the magic words of power, of which Isis and the traditional Magician of the Tarot are both masters. When the name is spoken, it is as if a person's essence is being breathed and manifested, externalized in the world of form—like the magic from a magician's wand.

Isis's guile and trickery, as well as her magical ability, is found on the *Contendings of Horus and Set*, from the *Papyrus Chester Beatty I* (twelfth century BCE), in which uncle and nephew fight for the rulership of Egypt in the absence of Osiris. Set believed that as the brother of the deceased king, he should rule in his place, but Horus believed that as the son of Osiris he was the natural successor and heir. Isis, of course, took the side of her son, and her bias at the council of the gods to discuss the matter caused them to ban her from all further proceedings. When all the gods, including Horus and Set, went to a deserted island to further discuss the matter and seek a resolution, the boatman to the island was told not to allow a woman like Isis across the river. So Isis bribed the boatman and shape-shifted into a beautiful young woman when she reached the island. There, she found Set and seduced him with honeyed words and beautiful eyes, and when he desired her she fell into tears, explaining her worry: that her husband had been killed by his brother, who came to their home and usurped her husband's position, taking her son's birthright and the ownership of their farm. Set, seeking her beauty, consoled her and stated that the brother was a scoundrel and that ownership of the farm obviously belonged to the rightful heir to the dead man's property. At this, Isis turned into a bird and flew up into the sky, crying out to the gods that Set had admitted that Horus should rule Egypt in his father's place. Later, when Set tried to sexually dominate Horus, Isis advised her son to catch Set's phallus and semen in his hand, at which she threw the semen into a river. She then told her son to produce his own semen, and sprinkled it upon the only food that Set ate: lettuces. When Set proudly declared to the council of the gods that Horus could not rule, because he had dominated him sexually, the gods tested the claim. They called for the semen of Set to come out, but instead of emanating from Horus, it came from the river. Horus then stated that instead *he* had performed the deed on Set, and when his semen was called forth, it came straight from Set's belly. Thus, the council of the gods gave the rulership of Egypt to Horus.

Perhaps the most beautiful depiction of Isis as the powerful goddess of all comes from the Late Antique period, in the writings of Lucius Apuleius, who may have been an initiate in the cult of Isis. In his *Metamorphoses* he described praying to Isis and having a vision of her:

> You see me here, Lucius, in answer to your prayer. I am Nature, the universal Mother, mistress of all the elements, primordial child of time, sovereign of all things spiritual, queen of the dead, queen also of the immortals, the single manifestation of all gods and goddesses that are. My nod governs the shining heights of Heaven, the wholesome sea-breezes, the lamentable silences of the world below. Though I am worshipped in many aspects, known by countless names, and propitiated with all manner of different rites, yet the whole round Earth venerates me. The primeval Phrygians call me Pessinuntica, Mother of the gods; the Athenians, sprung from their own soil, call me Cecropian Artemis; for the islanders of Cyprus I am Paphian Aphrodite; for the archers of Crete I am Dictynna; for the trilingual Sicilians, Stygian Proserpine; and for the Eleusinians their ancient Mother of the Corn.
>
> Some know me as Juno, some as Bellona of the Battles; others as Hecate, others again as Rhamnubia, but both races of Ethiopians, whose lands the morning sun first shines upon, and the Egyptians who excel in ancient learning and worship me with ceremonies proper to my godhead, call me by my true name, namely, Queen Isis (Graves 1951).

. . . *So below*

DIVINATORY MEANINGS

In a reading, The Magician often refers to a manifestation of something through an act of will and energy, directed and pure. It is the primary thrust of action and spark of inspiration, united with the access to and manipulation of resources (whether they are physical or metaphorical) that leads to the culmination of one's desire. This card states that the querent has everything they need to achieve their goal, but they must know how to apply those resources, how to control the situation, and where to direct their focus and energy. If they apply their will to the matter, very little can get in their way. This card is a bringer of power—not power over others, but power to act and do, in a proactive manner. When in a tough spot, The Magician can conjure something out of nothing, creating form from formlessness and order from chaos.

However, The Magician is not always as it seems, for this card suggests that there may be more subtle, cunning, and sneaky ways for the querent to achieve their goals. While there is an aspect of the charlatan here when the card is negatively aspected, it can also indicate the application of wit, trickery, and guile as the means to the desired end. The querent should note that their words have as much power as their actions, and that what they put out into the world, no matter how trivial, gains some type of reality. As such, they have complete control over their universe, and are standing right at the center of it. This card can also indicate an ego or focus on the self—at times this can be positive, but at others times it can become selfish and self-centered, ignoring the needs of others.

If The Magician appears in relation to a project, goal, or creative pursuit, it is extremely beneficial for the querent, indicating that as long as the querent applies the resources at hand correctly and puts their will, focus, and energy toward the goal, they will achieve it and arrive at completion and manifestation.

KEYWORDS

Drive; manifestation; resources; trickery, guile, cunning; magic; focus; will; creation; inspiration; ego; personality; giving order to chaos and form to formlessness

II THE HIGH PRIESTESS

Sophia
GNOSTIC CHRISTIAN; BIBLICAL

Within her seven-pillared temple, Sophia—Wisdom—is seated upon the throne of the world. She wears white for her purity, but the veil that covers her head and eyes is blue and crowned with stars. The light from her halo illuminates her wings, and she holds out communion bread in an offering of spiritual nourishment. Upon her lap is a closed holy text, and not quite there is the glowing communion chalice or grail. A purple veil is suspended behind her, covering the entrance or exit to the temple, and in her small, mysterious smile is complete silence and the promise of mystery.

As above . . .

GODDESSES AND SYMBOLS

The figure of Sophia has undergone many reimaginings over the years. Within various traditions she is seen as a saint, a goddess, a spiritual being that is part of the Christian Holy Trinity, a personification of wisdom, the World-Soul, and the mother or the creator of the world. Some of her earliest appearances are found in the Old Testament, in which she is presented as a female personification of wisdom, urging people to seek her out and making herself available to all who would diligently strive toward her:

> Choose my instruction instead of silver,
>
> knowledge rather than choice gold,
>
> for wisdom is more precious than rubies,
>
> and nothing you desire can compare with her.
>
> I, wisdom, dwell together with prudence;
>
> I possess knowledge and discretion.
>
> To fear the Lord is to hate evil;
>
> I hate pride and arrogance,
>
> evil behavior and perverse speech.
>
> Counsel and sound judgment are mine;
>
> I have insight, I have power.

By me kings reign

and rulers issue decrees that are just;

by me princes govern,

and nobles—all who rule on Earth.

I love those who love me,

and those who seek me find me (Proverbs 8:10–17, NIV).

In the same text, Sophia is shown in a protective role over those who seek her out:

Get wisdom, get understanding; do not forget my words or turn away from them. Do not forsake wisdom, and she will protect you; love her, and she will watch over you" (Proverbs 4:5–6, NIV). Elsewhere in the Old Testament she is portrayed as the pure breath of God, making her a fundamental part of creation. She is "so pure that she penetrates everything. She is a breath of God's power—a pure and radiant stream of glory from the Almighty (Wisdom 7:24–25, NIV).

It is symbolically appropriate that Sophia is also often described as a virgin, since the wisdom she brings is completely holy and pure, with the greatest potential. It is symbolized in the card image of the High Priestess by the veil that covers the entrance (or exit) of the temple, protecting the mysteries. In protecting them, Sophia is also conveying them to us—if they were revealed for all to see, they would no longer be mysteries. The Old Testament also tells us that Sophia was created before the world came into being, and helped God create it as a cobuilder:

The Lord brought me forth as the first of his works, before his deeds of old; I was formed long ages ago, at the very beginning, when the world came to be. . . . I was there when he set the heavens in place, when he marked out the horizon on the face of the deep, when he established the clouds above and fixed securely the fountains of the deep, when he gave the sea its boundary so the waters would not overstep his command, and when he marked out the foundations of the Earth. Then I was constantly at his side. I was filled with delight day after day, rejoicing always in his presence, rejoicing in his whole world and delighting in mankind (Proverbs 8:22–31).

This Old Testament Sophia has "built her house; she has set up its seven pillars," and she has "prepared her meat and mixed her wine; she has also set her table. She has sent out her servants, and she calls from the highest points of the city" (Proverbs 9:1–3). This is a female personification of holy Wisdom, a companion of God the creator, calling to us to seek her out and know her, welcoming all. The seven pillars of her house are symbolic of many things: the seven days of the week, the seven classical planets, or the seven graces of the spirit. In the eighth century CE, the seven pillars of wisdom were also known as the handmaidens of Sophia and were called Grammar,

Rhetoric, Dialectic, Arithmetic, Geometry, Music, and Astronomy, representing various kinds of knowledge.

Sophia is also a figure found in early Gnostic Christian thought. In the second century CE, the Valentinian movement was becoming a threat to the Christianity of St. Paul and offered a different cosmological view to that which would become canonical Christian belief. In the Valentinian account of creation (found in the *Apocryphon of John*, subtitled "The Revelation of the Mysteries Hidden in Silence"), God was an ineffable father who dwelt alone in the pleroma and created a series of thirty aeons consisting of fifteen pairs of masculine and feminine attributes or abstract concepts, such as Henosis (Union) and Makaria (Happiness). The lowest of these aeons was Sophia, and she longed to create life without input from her masculine partner. She did so, but the being she created was deformed and ignorant, so she hid it in a cloud, away from the sight of God and the other aeons. This being was named Yaldabaoth and would go on to create the world in six days, resting on the seventh, and creating humankind in his image. Meanwhile, Sophia "came down in innocence in order to rectify her deficiency. Therefore she was called Life, which is the mother of the living, by the foreknowledge of the sovereignty of heaven. And through her they have tasted the perfect Knowledge" (Robinson 1990, 118).

In this Gnostic cosmology, Sophia was also known as Zoe (life), Ennoia (thought), Pronoia (forethought), Sige (silence), and Eidea (image), and in the first century CE, Philo Judaeus identified her as mother of the divine Logos (word) and as Isis, mother of Horus. Although Philo followed biblical tradition in according primacy to the father god as creator and treating the divine mother—Sophia—as his attribute or emanation, he nevertheless described this god as the husband of Wisdom (Long 1992, 46, 162; Patai 1990, 98). Sophia was almost universally a creatrix, either by herself or alongside God, Mother Wisdom who nurtured humankind, so it is not surprising that the alchemical tradition of the Middle Ages depicted her as the World-Soul, nourishing all facets of creation. In the seventeenth century, she was described by Gottfried Arnold similarly:

> Now Sophia sends the soul, after all necessary discipline and first milk-nourishment, also stronger food, so that it may be nourished and wander in the new life. Because after the inward ear is opened through so many knockings within, and is made ready to receive, the heart is also humbled, and the will bound: she willingly lays out her treasures in a unified heart even more, and entrusts even more important things than one might have hoped (Versluis 2000, 118).

The wisdom Sophia offers is not the same as knowledge, but true inner wisdom, gained through "knocking" on the inner doors of the self. The temple entrance at which Sophia sits is the mystery of the self. However, this inner wisdom cannot be found in talking, proclamations, or a busy mind, but rather in silence. A third-century CE text, *Thunder, Perfect Mind*, found in the Nag Hammadi library in 1945 among other Gnostic writings, seems to be spoken by Sophia as Sige—Silence. In this text the reader is presented with paradox after paradox, designed to eventually bring the mind to a standstill and therefore silence. The card image shows two of these paradoxes carved above and below Sophia:

I am the hearing which is attainable to everyone, and the speech which cannot be grasped. I am a mute who does not speak, and great is my multitude of words (Robinson 1990, 301).

The same text also says:

I am the silence that is incomprehensible
and the idea whose remembrance is frequent.
I am the voice whose sound is manifold
and the word whose appearance is multiple. . . .
I am control and the uncontrollable.
I am the union and the dissolution.
I am the one below,
and they come up to me.
I am the judgment and the acquittal.
I, I am sinless,
and the root on sin derives from me (Robinson 1990, 298, 301).

This paradoxical text spoken by Mother Wisdom herself is rather like the old Buddhist meditation upon the "sound" of one hand clapping. When the mind realizes that the answer is paradoxical, it reaches a tiny, still point of nothingness and silence into which inner wisdom can flow.

. . . So below

DIVINATORY MEANINGS

The High Priestess is a card that contains a variety of abstract and complex concepts, as well as dense symbolism to be interpreted. It often appears in a reading to point to a need for silence or pause instead of discussion or action; it suggests that answers are to be found within the querent and that they may know the answer to their question already. Sometimes it can indicate the presence of questions that are difficult to answer or pose a problem of paradox or complexity.

Often, when the High Priestess appears in a reading, it indicates all things concerning intuition and inner wisdom, rather than logical thought and exoteric knowledge. As such it might indicate practices such as meditation, reflection, and techniques to improve psychic ability and the ability to sense auras, energy, or spirits. The realm of the High Priestess is that of divination of all kinds, such as Tarot, runes, mediumship, and oracles, since these are all mysterious, occult, and magical means of obtaining answers that many would consider otherwise unobtainable. In certain circumstances this card may also represent prophetic or oracular statements, channeling, and any other way in which messages are received from the "otherworld."

Sometimes this card, with its closed book and emphasis on silence, advises the querent to keep something to themselves. This may manifest in any area of life, such as social relationships, work and business, projects, or family; it might also point to the mysteries and vows of silence within initiation into magical traditions or mystery religions.

In a relationship reading, the High Priestess can represent a feminine force or figure, and points to the power that can be found in receptivity. It suggests that the querent might consider taking a more passive role, doing less talking in a relationship and more listening, and allowing other people a chance to take the lead. If the querent is not currently in a relationship, the appearance of this card suggests this will remain the same for a while yet. Socially, the querent might find this card indicating a friend or contact that is important to the situation, and in a family matter it might point to a sister or mother, albeit a distant one. It can also indicate that somebody in a friendship or social circle—perhaps the querent—needs to take time to themselves and may be more of an introvert than an extrovert.

For a work or business situation, this card is difficult to read. If the querent is seeking advice then it suggests they already know the answer and are now simply seeking confirmation: They should act upon their intuition and gut instinct and be prepared to adapt and flow around the situation or any obstacles.

When negatively aspected, the High Priestess can indicate a person who is so quiet and withdrawn that they do not feel they can voice their opinions. They think very little of themselves and are so introverted that it prevents them from moving forward, making friends, or asking for what they need and want. When accompanied by the Moon, this card points to the female body as well as to the spiritual-emotional world.

In a general sense, this card in a reading is the embodiment of wisdom, so it often brings a message concerning the various ways in which the querent might seek, find, and manifest wisdom.

KEYWORDS

Silence; wisdom; mystery; knowledge; understanding; quiet; reflection, contemplation, introspection; introversion; spiritual world; vows of secrecy; secrets; receptivity; oracles, prophecy; answers

III THE EMPRESS

Xōchiquetzal
AZTEC

Through a verdant landscape, surrounded by colorful flowers and fruiting trees, Xōchiquetzal, the Aztec goddess of love, pleasure, sensuality, childbirth, and crafts, walks bearing a child on her hips. Her belly is swollen with a full pregnancy, her skin is kissed by the sun, and she is decorated with precious metals and jewels that have been skillfully crafted. The field behind her is filled with marigolds, her sacred flower, and around her the plumed bird and the butterfly hover, animal companions to this goddess. The translucent butterfly wings on her back remind us of her sacred animal and the beauty of the natural world all around us, inspiring us to create beauty in our turn.

As above . . .

GODDESSES AND SYMBOLS

The term "Aztec" refers to different ethnic groups of people found in central Mexico, many of whom spoke the Nahuatl language. We know a lot about these people from the texts (called codices) produced after the Spanish conquest of Mexico in the sixteenth century, but only a few preconquest codices have survived. These earlier codices are pictorial, rather than textual, and while the postconquest codices continued this pictorial tradition, most of them also included writing and glosses. As such, it is likely that some of the postconquest codices, and therefore the information we have about the mythology of the Aztecs, are influenced by Christian religious ideas.

Xōchiquetzal was the Aztec goddess of love, pleasure, sensuality, childbirth, and crafts. Her name translates from Nahuatl as "Precious Feather Flower," "Flower Feather," or "Plumed Serpent Flower," from *quetzal* ("plumed bird," "precious feather") and *xōchitl* ("flower"). She was the twin sister of the god Xōchipilli, who shares part of Xōchiquetzal's name, his full name translating as "Flower Prince" or "Flower Child." These siblings also shared similar attributes: They both ruled over crafts and craftspeople, flowers, and beauty, but while Xōchipilli's rulership extended to dance, art, and song, Xōchiquetzal's extended to sex and pleasure, and all that they entail. She seems to have shared with other goddesses the role of fertility goddess, watching over women in childbirth and giving fertility to the land and humans; for instance, Tlazōlteōtl, the goddess of passion, sexuality, and taboos, shared many features of Xōchiquetzal. While Xōchiquetzal ruled over fertility, it becomes clear through the codices that she was not just a mother, but primarily a lover, expressing the act of intercourse for pleasure and fun instead of just procreation. One scholar commented on Tlazōlteōtl and Xōchiquetzal:

> Mesoamerican spiritual sexuality is revealed especially in the cult of these two goddesses. Xochiquetzal, the goddess of lovers, was the patroness of ritual sexual relations. . . . With this goddess, the emphasis is on amorous activity rather than on fertility. She protected illicit sexual relationships and was the patroness of the priestesses chosen to perform ritual sexual relations (Marcos 1992, 167).

It is this sensual side of her personality that may be the cause of the main myth concerning Xōchiquetzal, told in many different codices. According to the *Codex Telleriano-Remensis*, before the world as we know it came into being, there was a beautiful paradise in the west called Tamoanchan. The gods and goddesses lived there, and it was there too that the first couple was created. There was a tree in Tamoanchan called Xochitlicacan ("Flowering Tree"), and the myth describes Xōchiquetzal plucking the blossom from this tree, causing it to shatter. Following this, Xōchiquetzal was banished to Earth. It has become clear from scholarly studies of the myth that this plucking of blossom was actually an illicit sexual relationship between Xōchiquetzal and a god (Graulich et al. 1983, 575–88). This god may have been Tezcatlipoca, who seduced Xōchiquetzal while disguised as an animal (*Codex Telleriano-Remensis*, trans. in Núñez 1964, plates 30–31). The similarities between this myth and the Christian tale of Eve plucking the forbidden fruit from the Tree of Knowledge are interesting, especially since this act in both cases causes the expulsion from paradise, the bringing of death to the world, and the bringing of life: From Eve's act, humankind was born, and from Xōchiquetzal's act of illicit sexual pleasure / plucking of flowers, she gave birth to the god Centeōtl, maize. Centeōtl is described as descending to Earth and dying as soon as he arrived, which may be an allusion to the harvesting of maize and the agricultural cycle.

However, the paternity of Centeōtl is not agreed upon by all the codices, since elsewhere he is born from prohibited intercourse (called "plucking blossoms from a tree") between Xōchiquetzal, representative of Earth, and Piltzintecuhtli, representative of the sun (Graulich 1989, 46). This relationship between Earth and Sun is clearly one where pleasure becomes fertility and mimics the growth of vegetation. The only feature missing is rain, although some scholars identify Xōchiquetzal as a goddess of water as well.

In other accounts of the time in Tamoanchan, Xōchiquetzal's role brings creation and fertility in a less direct way. One story tells of a divine couple, Oxomoco and Cipactonal, who had a son, Piltzintecuhtli (Xōchiquetzal's husband in some stories, son in others). They took a hair from Xōchiquetzal's head to create from it a wife for their son. This way, Xochiquetzal indirectly ensured that Piltzintecuhtli could procreate and produce viable offspring.

Although the central myth of Xōchiquetzal's illicit relationship with Tezcatlipoca commonly places her in the role of the seduced rather than the seducer, it seems that she was sometimes the one who seduced others, once again highlighting her sensuality and beauty. For instance, in the *Codex Laud* there is an image of her, naked, tempting Quetzalcoatl into intercourse (Mundkur et al. 1976, 430).

So full of sensuality and sexual pleasure is Xōchiquetzal that some sources describe flowers being born from her genitalia (such as in the *Codex Magliabecchiano*, trans. in Anders 1970, verse 60). Many scholars suggest that she not only ruled over the world of love and pleasure but that she was also the patron of prostitutes, possibly even sacred prostitutes (Torquemada 1969, 2:299). One image of her, from the *Codex Borbonicus* (written either shortly before or shortly after the Spanish conquest), shows her with an assistant, seated on a chair decked with animal skins. Flowers come out of her mouth, and a snake can be seen coming out from beneath her. Flowers also come from beneath her, and it is unclear if they are coming from beneath her seat or from her genitals, as the myths suggest. Her hair is covered with a plumed headdress, and she is adorned with ornate facial jewelry. This representation (found in the card image, carved into the tree behind Xōchiquetzal) is one of beauty, luxury, and sensuality. She brings with her riches and fertility, pleasure, and seduction. She represents sex for pleasure as well as for procreation, although it can be suggested that she primarily inspires the lust and desire for pleasure that leads to procreation. This luxury can further be seen on one Aztec calendar stone in which a fourth age of abundance and fertility was depicted, with Xōchiquetzal as its herald:

> The principal figure is Xochiquetzal descending from heaven with flowers (*Sochiquetzal idest essaltatione delle rose*). After this period had lasted 5042 years, a great famine is said to have intervened when nearly all the people perished. The cause of this calamity was vice (MacCurdy 1910, 487).

However, whenever something is created, it brings about the potential for its destruction. We come into life under pain of death, and Xōchiquetzal also reminds us of the tomb that is a necessity once we come from the womb. In the codices, she is said to be "the first to give birth and the first brave one to die heroically" (Durand-Forest and Graulich 1984, 134), or who "died in war." Scholars have noted that "women who died in childbirth... were compared to warriors dying in the capture of a prisoner" (Harrington 1988, 31). We know from the codices that there was a *veintena* (a month, or period of twenty days) that was probably dedicated to the spirits of dead children, and it seems that Xōchiquetzal played a protective role in this festival:

> Durin..., Tovar... and the Codex Magliabechiano... say that the *veintena* was dedicated to the dead children and Durin and Tovar even feel that it was a *small* festival for this particular reason. It is however a well-known fact that the diminutive only indicates a minor festival with respect to the following one. The illustrations of the codices Telleriano-Remensis and Vaticanus A represent a funerary bundle with a mask of Cihuacoatl-Chantico or Xochiquetzal, both Earth and fertility goddesses who died in childbirth. So we may suppose that the deceased celebrated during this "small" festival of the dead were essentially the "divine" or warrior women who died "heroically"; that is, in childbirth, and maybe also the children (Graulich 1989, 53).

Perhaps Xōchiquetzal, being a "heroic warrior" herself, watched over the spirits of the women who, like her, died in childbirth, and took the spirits of deceased children under her protection in the afterlife? Since she is said to have been the first to give birth, she is very close to the concerns of human women. She is even said to have been the first to menstruate:

> She is the first real woman, and it is from her that flowers are born: according to the *Codex Magliabecchiano* . . . , Quetzalcoatl masturbates and his semen is transformed into a bat that tears off a piece of the vulva of Xōchiquetzal. From this piece come flowers. The bat, an animal responsible for issues of blood—it is also the animal that decapitates, and in the codices Xochiquetzal is also associated with decapitations—is probably here creating the female sex and menstruation, for doubtless the flowers born from the torn-off piece symbolize menstrual blood (Durand-Forest and Graulich 1984, 134).

Although at first menstruation may seem in opposition to the concept of fertility and creativity, being a destruction of the womb lining, it is only through first menses that it is noted that a woman is capable of procreating. Symbolically speaking, blood is life, and menstrual blood is the symbol of creativity and fertility. This fertility and creativity clearly didn't extend only to the female reproductive cycle, since Xōchiquetzal was the patroness of craftspeople, those who create beauty in art and works of skill, who work raw materials into something useful or that brings beauty and pleasure, just as the agricultural cycle and the reproductive cycle transform raw matter into something fully formed, whether it is vegetation or a child, both of which Xōchiquetzal gave birth to.

We have two surviving hymns that mention Xōchiquetzal. The first is a two-line hymn dedicated to her that seems to suggest some sort of search for Xōchiquetzal performed ritually by priests, perhaps during a harvest festival or a ritual to bring fertility to the land:

> I, Xochiquetzal, go forth willingly to the dancing place by the water, going forth to the houses in Tamoanchan. Ye noble youths, ye priests who wept, seeking Xochiquetzal, go forth there where I am going (Brinton 1890, 41).

The second hymn that mentions her is for a different god but depicts Xōchiquetzal in the marketplace, where the crafts of skill and beauty are sold:

> She goes to the mart, they carry Xōchiquetzal to the mart; she speaks at Cholula; she startles my heart; she startles my heart; she has not finished, the priest knows her; where the merchants sell green jade earrings she is to be seen, in the place of wonders she is to be seen. Sleep, sleep, sleep, I fold my hands to sleep, I, O woman, sleep (Brinton 1890, 54).

Here, the woman who sleeps is Xōchiquetzal, but she is also said to be carried to the marketplace, perhaps suggesting that those who worship her carry her fertility and protection with them when they sell their crafts. The hymn also suggests that she is found not only in places where craftspeople are—where man-made creativity exists—but also in "the place of wonders"—the natural world in all its glory, which provides us with so much inspiration and raw material for shaping.

. . . So below

DIVINATORY MEANINGS

The Empress graces readings with her beauty, sensuality, creativity, and fertility. Like most goddesses of fertility, this card not only brings something into creation but also engages in the pleasurable act of the process itself. As such, The Empress often points to any projects that the querent is working on, particularly creative projects, and paints the querent as a nurturer and birth-giver to their goals and finished projects. A journey or project indicated by The Empress may feel to the querent like a child, as if they are growing it within themselves; it may be hard labor bringing it to term and into the world in the final stages, but it will be a thing of beauty and skill when it is done.

Sometimes The Empress acts as a doorway of creativity, indicating a time when the querent will receive a great deal of creative inspiration and ideas. All areas of the querent's life will be fertilized—emotional, spiritual, intellectual, and mundane. If the querent has any concerns about the beginnings of something, The Empress suggests that they need not worry, but instead they should be assured that inspiration will come their way and will be the doorway to a cascade of ideas and growth. If this card appears in a reading or position about money, career, work, or the home, it usually points to a time of abundance and plenty. Healthwise, it indicates excellent health and vitality; however, if the reading is for a woman and The Empress is accompanied by particularly negative cards, it may indicate health issues with her reproductive organs or cycle. Rarely, this card surrounded by certain other cards can indicate difficulty in conceiving or a miscarriage. However, if accompanied by cards that also bear attributes of fertility and virility, The Empress can point to pregnancy.

Often, this card indicates somebody who acts in a nurturing role toward the querent, or suggests that this is the role that the querent themselves has taken or must take on in order to progress or aid somebody. The Empress asks the querent to consider their own skills and creative processes: What do they want to create? What can they create? From where does their imagination derive most inspiration? What are they skilled at? How do they create beauty in their lives? This card also asks them to think of themselves as sensuous, beautiful beings, capable of giving great love and pleasure. The Empress always brings with her love, whether it is sexual, familial, or platonic love, or whether it is love of a created thing, love of a hobby or pastime, or love of a career. When everything else is in darkness, the Empress's love burns like a torch everlasting.

KEYWORDS

Fertility, fecundity; abundance; creativity; imagination; skill; crafts, art; beauty; pleasure; sexuality; sensuality; creation; children; motherhood, mothering; maternal instincts; nurturing; procreation, reproduction

IV THE CONSTRUCT
(THE EMPEROR)

Nüwa
CHINESE

In a time of chaos, when the Earth has been flooded and fires have raged across its surface, caused by warring gods seeking dominion, the snake-tailed goddess of order, Nüwa, puts an end to the chaos by establishing the four pillars of the world and reaffixing the heavens in their proper place, filling the holes created by the damage with five colored stones. Her dominion is vast, and her role crucial for the continuation of the order of Earth. By her hands humankind was molded from yellow clay and given social status; in her repairing of the heavens she restored temporal order; in every act of creation she established spatial order. Her skirts are the width of the sky, but her worship has dwindled to nothing more than the names of mountains . . .

As above . . .

GODDESSES AND SYMBOLS

Following the creative potency of The Empress, the role of The Construct is to maintain, repair, and provide the necessary support, foundations, and frameworks for the continued existence of a creation. The Construct, the name of which reminds us that it depends upon something previous for its existence—in this case, The Empress—does not itself create, but gives structure to chaos and purpose to potential. It is, nonetheless, just as vital as the Empress. Where she is primal and offers up the raw materials, The Construct gives them shape and sets them in their proper place. This order is not only established by The Construct but maintained, as the process of creating structure from chaos is never-ending.

In Chinese mythology, like so many other mythologies from around the world, a catastrophic flood covered the Earth prior to the establishment of the world order as we know it. The *Huainanzi*, an ancient Chinese text dated to the second century BCE, tells us that before current humans existed:

> the four limits [of the world] collapsed and the Nine Provinces split apart. Heaven did not completely cover the world, nor did the Earth support all things. Fires raged without going out, and water surged on without ceasing. Fierce beasts devoured the simple people, and birds of prey carried off old

and young alike. Thereupon Nü Gua smelted the five-colored stones to patch up the azure sky, cut off the turtle's legs to re-establish the four limits, and killed the black dragon to rescue Ji Province [the central of the Nine Provinces, which in this passage stands metonymically for the entirety of China]. She piled up ashes from reeds to halt the rampant waters. Thus the azure sky was patched, the four limits corrected, the rampant waters dried up, Ji Province restored to order, and the treacherous creatures died (*Huainanzi*, chapter 6, quoted in Lewis 2006, 111).

Nü Gua, also called Nüwa, Nü Kua, and Wahuang ("Empress Wa"), is thus credited with repairing the heavens that had been damaged by the conflict, holding back the waters of the flood, and creating pillars to delineate the limits of the Earth. The four legs of the giant turtle used to reestablish the four limits represent the four corners of the Earth and the four directions, as well as reminding us that the Construct is numerologically associated with the number 4 and its potent energy of foundation, stability, order, and structure.

The concept of Nüwa mending the heavens became an enduring theme of Chinese art. The five colored stones she used to repair the heavens are a potent symbol of the foundational elements of life—they represent the five elements and the Wu Xing (Five Phases, also called the Five Agents and the Five Movements, representing how the five elements feed each other in a sequence of mutual generation). They are the building blocks of order in the natural world, and therefore the primal origin of order in the human world. In the card image, they are not only different colors but also different shapes, specifically the five Platonic solids. In the myth, Nüwa first fused or smelted these stones before using them to repair the heavens. In doing so, she brought the phases back into harmony, therefore bringing the natural order of things back into harmony. The Five Phases also regulated temporal sequence so were indicators of time. The fusing of the five colored stones by Nüwa is also linked with the blending of five colored substances in the erection of the soil altar used in rituals for granting fiefs—"the proper ordering of such substances becomes fundamental to the imposition of *spatial* order on the world" (Lewis 2006, 112). Granting fiefs confers rulership and dominion over the recipient, in the same way that The Construct oversees and maintains these things and is concerned primarily with their establishment, structure, and control.

The smelting of the five colored stones appears in ancient Chinese texts about the forging of swords, which were always forged in pairs—one male and one female. This link between the process of mending the heavens and the process of forging swords reminds us of a fundamental aspect of The Construct: war. As the active masculine, and being associated with the warlike zodiac sign Aries (which is ruled by the planet named after the Roman god of war, Mars), The Construct is at home in battle and sounds a call to arms to conquer, protect, and expand. Indeed, the poet Ch'in T'ao-yü tells us that Nüwa's dominion is vast: Her "gauzy skirt, a hundred feet long, suspended over the Hsiang and Kiang, gives its color to the hills" (Schafer 1973, 72) (a hundred feet is a traditional measurement of celestial distance).

Although Nüwa cannot be credited with the creation of the world, she is said to have created humankind as we know it following her mending of the heavens and reestablishment of order. Qu Yuan in the *Chu Ci* (fourth/third century BCE) and the poet Li Po in *Li T'ai-po wen chi* (eighth century CE), among others, said that she shaped humans out of the yellow earth and gave them the ability to procreate. Hsu Shen, a Chinese scholar of the second century CE, called her the "Transformer of the Myriad Creatures," granting her a creative power to give form to raw material (Schafer 1973, 31). In a late Eastern Han version of this myth, *Fengsu Tongyi*, Nüwa grew bored of the process of creation since it was taking too long, so instead of making humans from yellow mud individually, she crafted rope with many ends, all of which she dipped into the mud simultaneously in a mythical version of batch production (Lewis 2006, 120). The humans individually made from the yellow earth were those of higher social order, while the mass-produced humans were of lower social orders. Thus, Nüwa established social hierarchy. Like The Construct, Nüwa holds that everything has its place in the order of the world.

Images of Nüwa often depict her with the tail of a snake or dragon. Her tail is often entwined with that of her husband's, Fu Xi, who is also half human, half snake. Fu Xi is credited with creating the eight trigrams in order to gain mastery of the world, and is said to be the originator of the I Ching. Like his wife, he brought order and structure to chaos. As a pair, they often appear holding their respective symbols—he the carpenter's square and she the compass. These items provide a key to the understanding of The Construct:

> The compass and carpenter's square have symbolized fixed standards and rules that impose order on unruly matter. As such they are clearly appropriate to deities who were credited with the invention of kingship and of social hierarchy as well as the restoration of ordered space out of the chaos of the flood. The presence of these tools in the images placed in a tomb or shrine would serve to maintain proper order, both natural and social (Lewis 2006, 125–26).

. . . *So below*

DIVINATORY MEANINGS

The Construct provides a stabilizing and foundational force in the Tarot, offering to impose structure and order on chaos and establishing the frameworks within which progress may be made. Despite this fundamental and manifest energy, it can nevertheless be an abstract card in a reading, with its meaning being influenced by the questions and surrounding cards. Generally, this card signifies an area over which the querent has dominion, something over which they rule or have authority; sometimes it can indicate somebody who has authority over them or a prominent sphere of their life. Often, it indicates a paternal figure for the querent, or their own role as parent and guiding hand, offering structure and support to others.

Often, the Construct asks the querent how they can impose order on a situation, remove forces that are creating chaos, and establish a firm foundation from which to move forward. Sometimes it advises the querent that this foundation and structure may be found in those with authority, so they might look externally for answers.

Organizations and regulatory bodies can also be sought out for help and support. Anything concerning rules and boundaries is indicated by this card.

In readings about power dynamics and social structure, The Construct may suggest that the querent needs to establish their own power and authority or place themselves in a position of control and leadership. Because this card has an organizing role, it calls upon the querent to likewise be the organizer of a group. Thus, it may point to organizing and running events, a team, or a process. It may also indicate somebody who is the sole provider of a family and thus takes on all the roles of authority, structure, and care. However, The Construct's warlike quality and need to dominate can sometimes have a negative impact on relationships, and it can signify an overdomineering friend or partner, a micromanaging boss or manager, or a process or system that leaves no room for flexibility, creativity, or innovation. Negatively aspected, The Construct can indicate that the foundations for progress are missing, or that a plan has been executed poorly. It can also suggest that support networks are not in place.

In a business reading, this card is often positive. The stable and orderly active force of The Construct brings results to business ventures and returns on investments. In health readings, when surrounded by cards indicating blockages or difficulty, it can indicate specifically male health problems but otherwise suggests good health and an active lifestyle. In issues of self-improvement and spirituality it might indicate self-control and discipline. In an advisory position it may also recommend that the querent take a more active, even aggressive, approach to a situation.

KEYWORDS

Order; establishing structure; putting rules and boundaries in place; laying down a foundation; giving order to chaos; organization; regulation; limitations; dominion; authority; rulership; aggression; an active approach; a paternal figure

V THE HIEROPHANT

St. Mary Magdalene
CHRISTIAN

A wooden boat makes land on the shores of Saintes-Maries-de-la-Mer, bearing the three Marys of the region's folklore and their wisdom to a new world. Mary Salome, clothed in red, leans out of one side of the boat expectantly; another, Mary of Jacob, gently cradles an alabaster jar; the Mary in the center is the Magdalene herself, holding the book of wisdom and bearing a key to the mysteries upon her breast. Her right hand is held up in benediction, and holy light radiates from her. Together they have brought their faith and the teachings of the Rabbi, Jesus of Nazareth, to these shores, and it is here they will found their new church, revealing the sacred to all.

As above . . .

GODDESSES AND SYMBOLS

A great deal has been written about Mary Magdalene over the centuries, and a significant volume of artwork has depicted her in a variety of garbs, hairstyles, poses, and attitudes. She has been displayed as the repentant sinner, the sacred harlot, the woman with the alabaster jar, the lover of Christ, the mother of the Merovingian line, the Apostle to the Apostles, and the woman possessed by seven demons. Her Roman Catholic feast day is celebrated on July 22, and her discovery of Jesus's empty tomb after his crucifixion is commemorated on April 24.

Certainly the story and meaning of the Magdalene has shifted over the ages, and her identity conflated and confused with other women and Marys of the gospels. Here, we present her as The Hierophant, a title given to somebody who interprets sacred mysteries or esoteric principles. The term itself comes from the Greek *ta hiera* ("the sacred") and *phainein* ("to show") and means "revealer of the sacred." It is into this role—as Apostle to the Apostles and first witness to the resurrection of Jesus—that we place Mary Magdalene and the women who, according to folklore, accompanied her to the shores of France and preached the teachings of Jesus in those new lands. As Hierophant they are teachers, advisors, holders of wisdom, and guides to the mysteries.

The term "apostle" in the original Greek of the New Testament is also used to mean "delegate," "envoy," or "messenger" (Haskins 1993, 58). It comes from *apostello*—to send away or order somebody to go to an appointed place. An apostle in Christian religion indicates an important early teacher, disciple, and advocate for the faith and is commonly given to the twelve apostles of Christ—all men. These were the first and most faithful of Jesus's followers before his crucifixion, and the first to go out and spread the message of his resurrection. As such, the title given to Mary Magdalene—"Apostle to the Apostles"—by Hippolytus of Rome in the third century is a significant one, indicating a primacy of understanding and teaching of the faith. The gospels also have Mary Magdalene being the first to be charged with the ministry of proclaiming the Christian message, having been the first to witness Jesus's empty tomb and resurrection (John 20:17–18, Luke 24:10, and Mark 16:9–10). As the first witness to these mysteries, Mary Magdalene was the first to perceive the foundations of Christian belief. Although the gospels list various other women as being present with Mary Magdalene at the discoveries (Mary Salome, Joanna, Mary Clopas, and Mary mother of James), it is Mary Magdalene who is given the special attention and title.

Not only the canonical gospels but Gnostic writings grant to Mary Magdalene a special place as apostle, teacher, and revealer of the sacred. In the *Gospel of Mary*, written in the fifth century, it is Mary Magdalene who encourages the terrified disciples and is asked to tell them of Jesus's words. She does so by speaking of a vision she has received and what it reveals, before falling silent (Robinson 1990, 525–26). In *The Sophia of Jesus Christ*, she is called Mariamme and was the key female disciple in the inner circle of disciples. *The Dialogue of the Saviour* singles her out as having a particularly deep understanding of the teachings of Jesus, who describes her as "a woman who knew the All"; he also states that she "reveal[s] the greatness of the Revealer" (Ruether 2005, 123). The *Pistis Sophia*, dating to the third or fourth century CE, describes her as "the inheritor of Light." In this text, Mary Magdalene becomes an aspect of the Sophia (wisdom) of God—the manifestation and delivery of faith-wisdom. She asks thirty-nine of the forty-two questions posed to Jesus by the disciples, and her questions elicit wisdom and further explanation from him. In this, she acts as a coteacher with Jesus. Susan Haskins described her in this text as "a figure who, even if not actually here the symbol of divine Wisdom, in seeking and imparting knowledge about the Pistis Sophia, becomes the handmaiden and sometimes alter ego to the symbol of divine Wisdom herself" (Haskins 1993, 44). It is no accident that in this deck, the High Priestess card is Sophia herself, the wisdom of God, for these two cards are often seen as a pair in the Tarot pack, representing different types of wisdom, teaching, and authority. In the eyes of the Gnostic Christians of the first few centuries, Mary Magdalene was clearly an important figure. The *Gospel of Phillip* states that she was "the companion of the saviour" and that he "loved Mary more than all the disciples" (Robinson 1990, 148). In the modern period she was seen as Ecclesia, the church, just as Mary mother of Christ was (Murray 1975, 148).

It was in the Merovingian period that the focus of Mary Magdalene as teacher and disciple shifted to that of the repentant prostitute—a reputation that remains with her to this day—when Gregory the Great delivered a homily on the Gospel of Luke. Therein he conflated Mary Magdalene with the Mary from whom seven devils were driven out in the Gospel of Mark and the Mary that the Gospel of John called a sinful woman and the woman who wept over Jesus's feet and dried them with her hair (Erhardt and Morris 2012, 200). Even in this confused identity, however, the Magdalene continued to teach and guide the faithful: As the repentant sinner and sinful woman turned to a holy life, she guided people to a better life and toward a focus on God.

Indeed, a devout following arose around her in the eleventh century and continues to this day. According to the local legends of Saintes-Maries-de-la-Mer in the Camargue, France—as the name of the place suggests—Mary Magdalene and two other Marys arrived in a boat having set sail from Alexandria, Egypt, following the death of Jesus. They brought with them the teachings of Jesus and helped spread Christianity in France. Today, Saintes-Maries-de-la-Mer is a site of religious pilgrimage for the Roma, who venerate St. Sarah (also called Sarah-la-Kali—Sarah the Black), a dark-skinned woman who was variously the Egyptian servant of the three Marys and a local who welcomed them off the boat (McDowell 1970, 38–57).

According to more modern legends, Mary Magdalene also brought something else with her to the shores of France—the blood of Christ himself, hidden in her womb in the form of a child. However, this legend has been conclusively demonstrated to be far more fiction than fact (Ehrman 2004). In fact, the focus on Mary Magdalene should be less about whether she was married to Jesus / his lover / the mother of his child, as many modern commentators have theorized, because, quite simply, her worth is not dependent on marriage to a man but is instead about her role and symbolism in spreading the word of this new religion to new shores, revealing the sacred to others, and preaching. Regardless of the truth or falsehood of the legends about her relationship with Jesus, however, it is a fact that Mary Magdalene has inspired tales that set her as a founder and revealer of the sacred, a teacher, and a guide. In the Eastern Orthodox church, a common legend tells of her visit to Rome to preach the gospel to the emperor Tiberius. Tiberius claimed that Christ had no more risen than the egg on his table was red. Mary picked up the egg, which immediately turned red in her hand.

As revealer of the Revealer, inheritor of the Light, Apostle to the Apostles, and a woman who knew the All, Mary Magdalene has remained in the heart of the Western world and guided her devoted to a greater understanding of God. In this, she has revealed the sacred, interpreted the mysteries, and acted as intercessor between the mundane and spiritual worlds.

. . . So below

DIVINATORY MEANINGS

The Hierophant is a card that many people feel uncomfortable with, since it depicts tradition and authority. For many Western people on a nontraditional spiritual path, this authority was first experienced in religions and faiths that did not work for them or that placed outward riches above inner wisdom. In *Pistis Sophia*, however, The Hierophant's authority comes from that very inner wisdom, reminding us that this card is a twin of The High Priestess—the two represent different types of teaching and wisdom. In a reading, The Hierophant often represents an individual, process, or similar that acts as a teacher to the querent. This is usually, but not always, in a well-known and well-trodden tradition or path, as The Hierophant is a card of long memory and tried-and-tested methods. Often it indicates an advisor, confessor, confidante, and guide, though they are not only to be found in the spiritual life: School teachers, professors, non-fiction authors, lecturers, and anybody else that reveals knowledge to others, can be represented herein.

Sometimes The Hierophant refers to education in its many forms, though it is more likely to relate to formal education. It suggests that the querent seek traditional wisdom if they wish to find out what their best course of action is, or consult with somebody they trust. It can also indicate an intercession on the querent's behalf by somebody in authority.

In the spiritual realm, this card represents all the ways in which the divine can manifest and reveal itself, or be revealed. The Hierophant says that there are great mysteries to unfold and that the querent should look out there—rather than in here—to plumb their depths. Turning to the available literature, accepted teachings and the paths others have trod are all roads to greater understanding.

The Hierophant may appear in a reading to represent an institution, such as a government, university, or research institute. It holds within it the foundations of knowledge and offers the querent a solid foundation for wisdom. It also points to all things concerning memory and reminds the querent that society and the social circles in which we move can also be considered institutions, with their own particular values, ideologies, and mores.

Negatively aspected, this card represents the abuse of authority, power over others used to evil ends, incorrect teaching, wrong facts, a failure to base one's wisdom and learning on suitable foundations, and the rejection of traditions, ideologies, and values.

KEYWORDS

Teaching; received and accepted wisdom; tradition; institutions; solid foundations of knowledge; an authority figure; advice and intercession; memory; facts; education; the revelation of the sacred

VI THE SISTERS
(THE LOVERS)

The Wawilak Sisters
YOLNGU AUSTRALIAN ABORIGINE

Here is the Dreamtime, the time in the mythical past yet also recurring with every moment, in which all things began and became. Here the Wawilak Sisters are seated facing each other, singing the menstruation songs, singing the water songs, singing the sister songs, and as their voices join so does their menstrual flow. They are united in their purpose to prevent Yurlunggur, the Rainbow Serpent, from swallowing them, having smelled their blood, yet they are also reunited through blood and kinship to their divine point of origin, their homeland, their mother's blood, their ancestral unity. Above them, the serpent's jaws distend in readiness, and the sisters, separate still despite their sharedness, are one moment away from being reabsorbed by the sacred. Beneath them, translucent mermaid tails twitch gently: These are the tails of the Murinbungo women, the Aboriginal mermaids who, like their counterparts throughout the world, call out to any of their missing sisters so that they might remember their origin in the rivers and oceans and remember the missing parts of themselves before reuniting with them.

As above . . .

GODDESSES AND SYMBOLS

The Yolngu of northeastern Arnhem Land tell a version of the Rainbow Serpent myth that focuses on two human women, the Wawilak sisters. A number of different versions of this myth are told by different groups and interpreters, which is common in any study of Australian Aborigine myth. It is clear when one reads these tales (or listens to them, as they would have done originally in this oral tradition) that the power of these myths lies in their ability to be interpreted according to the needs of the listener. As such, while to some interpreters this story is one of the ritual oppression of women and of female biology being "dirty" or "taboo," the more prevalent theory is that it represents the initiation of ceremony, song, and ritual by the two women, their reunion with their origin and their union with each other in the bond of sisterhood, and the institution of their songs and rituals as necessity in Aboriginal life to this day.

In this tale (retold from the version given in Warner 1957, 254–59), the two sisters from Wawilak country had committed incest within their tribe, so they went on walkabout, and as they went they named all the animals, plants, and places of the land. One, the older, was carrying a child in her arms, and one carried a child in her belly.

After they had journeyed many miles, the younger sister felt the child moving inside her and knew its time had come, so they stopped to rest. As they rested, the older sister massaged her sister's abdomen and induced labor pains. The child, a son, was born there, and soon they moved on, traveling toward the sea. Finally, they stopped at a watering hole in the country they named Mirrirmina ("rock python's back"), where they made camp. The elder sister went to gather some bark to make a bed for the newborn, and as she did so, some of her menstrual blood fell into the waters of the Mirrirmina well. The great spirit, the serpent called Yurlunggur, smelled the blood and rose from his sleep in the well. When he saw the cause of the blood, he looked upon the Wawilak sisters and knew that they were of his clan, Dua, and knew they were sisters to him and their sons were nephews to him. He hissed, calling out for rain, so the sisters built a shelter and slept there. When they awoke, the rains had become heavy, and they knew something was wrong. The older one went outside to beat the ground with a stick and dance, while the younger stayed inside and sang. The older realized that Yurlunggur would come and swallow them, and she sang to tell him to leave them alone. First, she sang all the ritual songs that are today sung in the general camp, then she sang the taboo ritual songs of the Djungguan, then the Yiritja, the Marndiella, and the Ulmark, her songs becoming more taboo as she continued. The rain did not stop, and finally she sang the songs of menstruation. At this, the younger sister came out and began to dance outside, and her dances brought on her menstruation. Now that the two women were bleeding together, Yurlunggur crawled out of the watering hole and licked the women all over, then swallowed them whole along with their sons. Because they were of his clan, however, Yurlunggur felt sick and regurgitated them, unconscious, into an ants' nest. The ants crawled over their bodies and bit them, waking them up; upon seeing this, Yurlunggur swallowed them a second time. He journeyed back across the land to their homeland, the Wawilak country, where he regurgitated them one last time, their bodies becoming large stones that can still be seen today.

The tale does not end here. It continues with two Wawilak men arriving at the final scene to investigate the noises but finding nothing but rocks and blood. They gathered the blood in baskets and fell asleep. In their dreams, the sisters came to them and told them to remember the songs and dances that they were going to show them. They showed the men the ceremony songs and dances that had created the land as they walked, so that they may continue to create it anew. These songs and dances are still performed today.

The idea of a mythical journey across the land, singing it into being, is explored by Bruce Chatwin (1998) in his classic *The Songlines*, which shows that the Dreamtime sang the land into existence, and that when modern Australian Aborigines sing the ritual songs they (according to the myth) inherited from the Wawilak sisters, they are singing the songlines of the land anew, re-creating the Earth with every moment. The tale is one of origin and creation. The theme of incest at the beginning of the tale reiterates this: Sister joining with brother, while taboo in most cultures, is a mythic motif of reuniting with the Other and rediscovering one's origins. Siblings share the same parent and therefore, in myth, the same divine origin. It is this that the Sisters card is concerned with: reuniting with the source of origin. The myth of the Wawilak sisters is also about two sisters, who are united not only by sharing their blood of origin and tribal links but also by the process of menstruation and childbirth. This motif can be found in the tribal allegiance of the sisters and Yurlunggur, for he was of the same tribe, so swallowing them indicates symbolically that they returned to their origin. To be swallowed up is a powerful symbol of this return, particularly since Yurlunggur is associated with water and rains, and the primal waters in turn represent the womb whence we all come, and the ocean whence all life came. Finally, at the end of the myth, the sisters are literally returned to their point of origin: Yurlunggur regurgitates them in Wawilak country.

The sister's unity in menstruation is both taboo and sacred:

> It was when the two sisters were bleeding together that two things almost simultaneously happened: (1) they entered their little hut together; (2) they were swallowed alive and carried to the sky. The implication that the combination of their blood-flows—the connexion of womb-with-waterhole or womb-with-womb—constituted the force which carried off the Sisters to the other world. ... [I]n Aboriginal "swallowing and regurgitation" myths generally, the infesting and regurgitating organ is an immense vagina or womb (Knight 1983, 23).

This points to mutual recognition of shared commonality on an internal level, particularly since the process of menstruation in women who are close and live together often occurs at the same time, known as the McKlintock effect, after the scientist who noted it in 1971 (McKlintock 1971, 24–25). Anthropologically speaking, it has been suggested that this synchronization of menstrual cycles would have allowed women in earlier human communities to give birth and therefore nurture their young in the same cycles, so that if one woman was unable to feed her child, another who had birthed her own at the same time could help. Since many cultures also instituted a form of secret women's society in which they went away from the usual social setting during their bleeding, it may be suggested that this synchronicity of cycles allowed the women all-important time together to reunite parts of themselves and form stronger bonds with each other.

Chris Knight (1983) asked why, if the swallowing and regurgitating myth of the sisters is a symbolic return to the womb and reconnection with divine origin through the Other, it is represented as so traumatic to the sisters. He then stated that myths work on many levels and often mean one thing to the initiated and another to the uninitiated. If we recall Joseph Campbell's suggestion that myth has four possible functions (Campbell 2011, 609–23), we see what is happening on two different levels in the tale: As Knight suggests, the outer function of this myth may be a moral one, intended to instill social values regarding women and children, putting forward the menstrual cycle as impure—specifically that the blood and activity of menstruation should be kept away from watering holes. However, the inner meaning of the myth is that of reconstitution, reunion, and reconnection, and this is supported by the fact that in this myth, the Wawilak sisters institutionalized all the rituals, songs, and ceremonies necessary for tribal society to function.

Knight (1983, 24–25) also pointed out, as have several other commentators, that the act of the sisters' menstruation is mimicked in ritual and initiation by men, who in some parts of Australia will undergo subincision (a mutilation of the penis down the middle) to mimic the menstrual bleeding of women—in fact, some openly boast to having stolen these mysteries from women (Berndt and Berndt 1951, 55). In some parts of Australia, Aboriginal menfolk will also cut themselves during ceremonies, smearing each other in their blood, and in some cases singing the song of menstruation supposedly sung by the Wawilak sisters themselves, to achieve reunion with each other:

> In being enveloped with a coating of blood, the men are being "swallowed" by "the Snake" (defined as a kinsperson), and this sensation of "belonging," of being "at home," of being with bloodkin—is what it feels like to be "swallowed alive." It is like returning to the safety of the womb (Knight 1983, 24).

Another important feature of The Sisters is that of opposites, and therefore the ability to distinguish one thing from another. Without things being separate, no act of reunion can take place. It is essential to note, therefore, that it is the journey of the Wawilak sisters across the land that institutes the ability to discriminate between one thing and another, since they named everything as they walked—all the places, all the features, all the plants, all the animals. Before that, many of the tales say, animals were like humans and humans were like animals, with no difference between. In his studies, W. L. Warner was told that all the polarities in life, such as the seasonal contrasts, the tension between life and death, youth and age, night and day, are "all the fault of those two Wawilak sisters" (Warner 1957, 385). The powerful and sacred act of naming that occurs in nearly every mythology therefore creates separation from the point of origin, which then necessitates the reunion and eventual return to the point of origin that the sisters themselves underwent in their menstrual synchrony, in their swallowing by Yurlunggur, and in their return through regurgitation to their homeland.

In some versions of the tale we are given a scene of recognition of the bond between the two sisters, and it is this moment that is depicted in the card image—the moment when the two sisters are joined in recognizing their ability to reunite, and the moment just before they enter into complete reconnection with the divine by being swallowed by Yurlunggur:

> The sisters sat down, looking at each other, with their feet out and legs apart, and both menstruated. Each one made a loop of the other one's menstrual blood, after which they put the string loops around their necks (McCarthy 1960, 426).

The card image also shows the sisters with translucent mermaid tales, referring to another Aboriginal myth to which they are linked (Knight 1988, 238) and that points to reconnection and reunion with one's origin through the Other. The Mungamunga girls, or Murinbungo, are water women like mermaids, about whom a number of tales are told similar to European mermaid tales—a man falls in love with one, removes her from the sea/lake/river, and lives with her until she is able to return somehow to her home, her tail (which is often stolen), and her watery sisters (Robinson 1966, 61–66). When the Murinbungo return to the water, they "become merged in the corporate identity of their mother" (Knight 1988, 238).

DIVINATORY MEANINGS

The Sisters has a double meaning. First, since it is traditionally called the Lovers, it is a card that indicates a recognition of something shared between two people, no matter what their gender, which often manifests in romantic love. There are many cards in the Tarot that might point to a relationship in a reading, yet when The Sisters appears it says that this is not just a casual encounter but a relationship in which the partners are in harmony with each other, completing each other like two parts of the same whole. When lovers describe meeting their partner as "coming home," that is The Sisters. As such, this card often also points to the experience of finding the other half of oneself through other means, such as a spiritual experience, or of completing oneself through a passion.

On another level, The Sisters indicates a recognition of a way toward reunion with the divine, often through another person, but in other ways as well. It says that we must first be separated from our point of origin, our divine Other, in order to have a gap that we might then be able to cross. Without the distinction between one thing and another, we are unable to yearn for those things to be reunited. Thus, The Sisters is both the reunion and the traversing of the gap between one thing and another, as well as the necessity of the gap itself. As such, it sometimes advises the querent to learn to discriminate or set aside one thing from another, to discern and see differences so that they may facilitate a more effective move toward unity. It suggests that the best results for the current project or journey are to be found when different things aren't the same, when the querent plays upon their distinctive differences and uses them in harmony. Just like a lock and key, those differences are required to move forward and for things or people to work together.

Often, The Sisters appears at a time when the querent desires unity and reunion, and this often manifests through a desire for a relationship or love. If accompanied by cards of contracts and binding, it may also indicate a relationship becoming marriage. If it appears in a question specifically about a relationship, it is a great blessing, and in a reading concerning business, work, or money, it suggests that passion and desire will play a role in pushing the querent toward their goal, yet they must also learn to respect their coworkers' or business partners' differences. Each person involved in the situation has their own talents and strengths, and it is this—not their similarity to each other—that will be vital.

KEYWORDS

Love; passion; yearning; recognition of the Other; relationship; harmony; differences; separation leading to reunion; distinction, discrimination between things; desire; reconnection, reunion; return to origin

VII THE CHARIOT

Nike
GREEK

In a triumphal parade of victory, the Greek goddess Nike, charioteer of Zeus, champion of heroes, grasps the reins of two horses, one black and one white, firmly in one hand while raising aloft the wreath of conquest and victory in the other. Confetti and flowers shower her from well-wishers and celebrators, and she carries in a sack at her side a lyre for singing the praises of heroes and retelling their epic tales. Nike's wings are outspread triumphantly, and the wheels of her chariot move ever onward, the road to victory never ending.

As above . . .

GODDESSES AND SYMBOLS

O powerful Nike, by men desired, with adverse breasts to dreadful fury fired, thee I invoke, whose might alone can quell contending rage and molestation fell. 'Tis thine in battle to confer the crown, the victor's prize, the mark of sweet renown; for thou rulest all things, Nike divine! And glorious strife, and joyful shouts are thine. Come, mighty Goddess, and thy suppliant bless, with sparkling eyes, elated with success; may deeds illustrious thy protection claim, and find, led on by thee, immortal fame (Orphic Hymn 33, *To Nike*, trans. in Taylor 1792).

Nike, Greek goddess of victory, according to Hesiod, was the daughter of Styx (upon whose waters the gods swore oaths) and Pallas (or, in one telling, Ares), and the sister of Bia (Force), Cratus (Strength), and Zelos (Zeal) (Hesiod, *Theogony*, 383ff). The Romans called her Victoria, and one well-known sportswear brand has used this goddess's Greek name as their own, with a slogan to match her triumphant swiftness: "Just do it." Although Nike does not have any myths of her own, nor are there any stories in which she plays a major role, it is clear in the myths of the other Greek gods that she is vital to their endeavors.

The ancient writer Nonnus described Nike as driving Zeus's chariot into battle and leading him into battle against Typhon, whereas it was Eris who led Typhon into battle (Nonnus, *Dionysiaca* 2.358, 2.475). One might see here a comparison between the discord of Eris and the concord of Nike. But it seems that Nike wasn't just viewed as a goddess of victory in battle: she was also described by Nonnus as singing a song of victory for a newly wedded couple, preparing their bridal bed with song:

Nike (Victory) turned a tripling foot for the pleasure of Zeus, and stood as bridesmaid crying triumph for Kadmos the god's champion [who had assisted him in his conflict with the monster Typhon]; about the bridebed she wove the wedding song with her virgin voice, and moved her gliding steps in the pretty circles of the dance, while she fluttered her wings, shamesfast beside the wings of the Erotes (Loves) (Nonnus, *Dionysiaca* 5.88; trans. by Rouse in Nonnus 1989).

Nike was called upon to give victory in competition and games as well as battle, and so the Olympic games and similar contests were her territory. She is often depicted holding a wreath or palm frond, the traditional prizes for winners of the games. She was said to judge the games and any other contests:

Nike (Victory), giver of sweetness, to you the father, son of Ouranos, on his high bench has granted glorious honour, so that in gold-rich Olympos you stand beside Zeus and judge the outcome of prowess for immortals and mortals: be gracious, daughter of thick-tressed, right-judging Styx; it is thanks to you that Metapontion . . . is now filled with the celebrations and festivities of strong-limbed youths, and they sing the praises of the Pythian victor (Bacchylides, fragment 11, trans. in Campbell 1992).

It is recognized that Nike offers mortals the opportunity to win fame, reputation and achievement, even after death, as she provides them with victory that leads to such things:

By the altar of Zeus, best ruler, the flowers of glory-bringing Nike [i.e., the victory crown of the Games] nourish for men—a few mortals—a golden reputation conspicuous in their life-time always; and when the dark-blue cloud of death covers them there is left behind undying fame for the deed well done (Bacchylides, fragment 13; trans. in Campbell 1992).

In this sense, Nike offers victory as a means to an end, so that victory is not the only goal or aim, or the end of one's journey, but rather a stepping stone to further things. When one reaches the summit of a mountain, one is faced not with the view below but with the next higher peak. Since the journey to achievement is never really complete, Nike urges people on to victory, giving them the strength and force to carry on even when they do not see their own strength or ability. In one passage from Nonnus she is shown urging Zeus to fight against Typhon when he is about to give up, after Typhon had laid siege to Olympus, causing all the other gods to flee:

Zeus was alone, when Nike (Victory) came to comfort him, scoring the high paths of the air with her shoe. She had the form of Leto; and while she armed her father, she made him a speech full of reproaches with guileful lips (Nonnus, *Dionysiaca* 2.205; trans. by Rouse in Nonnus 1989).

Nike could be depicted with wings, such as the Nike of Samothrace that currently resides in the Louvre Museum, dating to the third/second century BCE, and another of her in the Louvre on an Attic amphora from the Late Classical period. However, she is also depicted at times without wings, as Nike Apteron. Pausanius suggested that the reason for wingless Nikes is because the sculptors did not want victory to escape from them (Pausanias, *Description of Greece* 3.15.7; trans. in Frazer 2010).

Nike is often linked to Athena, although there is much debate regarding this point among scholars. André Baudrillart (1894) stated that Nike was originally an abstraction from Athena, since Athena was originally the giver of good counsel (Boulaia), skill at craft (Ergane), and victory (Nike) (Harrison 2004, 366). An earlier mythologist, Ludwig Preller, stated that Nike had an independent character from her point of origin (Sikes 1895, 281), whereas Friedrich Imhoof-Blumer thought that Nike disappeared somewhat and did not have associations with battle until later in her development, but was revived with the Olympian games as a goddess of victory in games rather than war (Imhoof-Blumer 1876).

Although the image of Nike driving a chariot belongs to the archeology of this goddess (she is often depicted driving the chariot of Zeus), it also serves a symbolic function in the card image to remind us of the Greek philosopher Plato's analogy of the soul as a chariot drawn by two horses, one noble and one ignoble. Where one is wild and the other tame, they pull in different directions, and the charioteer has difficulty controlling them. In the same way, the soul of a human pulls in different directions, causing delays and obstacles for our evolution. If we can take firm control of our chariot and focus all aspects of our selves toward one goal, our journey toward completion will be swift and triumphant (Plato, *Phaedrus*, 245c–254e).

. . . *So below*

DIVINATORY MEANINGS

To see The Chariot in a reading is a blessing, particularly if the querent is currently finding themselves stuck in a rut, or moving toward completing a goal or achieving an ambition. This card assures the querent that whatever their goal or dream, success is at hand and possibly quicker than they expect—The Chariot brings swiftness and fast progress in its wake. Triumph and victory are the concerns of this card, so the querent is likely to experience events such as job promotions, pay rises, attainment of grades above what they expected, offers of university places or jobs, publishing contracts, a victory in contests or rivalry, or the attainment of a longed-for goal. Usually this card appears toward the end of a journey or quest to indicate the conclusion rather than the beginning of that journey or its inspiration.

With this card also comes the message of pure will and directed energy. The querent cannot let themselves become distracted from their purpose or goal but must direct everything at their disposal toward it. Focus is key to success.

At times, The Chariot appears in a reading to encourage the querent to action. If they are stuck, feeling stagnant, or fearing movement, The Chariot tells them that the only solution to break out of inaction is direct and certain action. They must move, whether it is physically or metaphorically. This card goads the querent into strength and focus of will toward their goal and urges them to stay their course. Sometimes The Chariot also advises that, luckily for the querent, the process and journey are already set in motion and are now an unstoppable force in the querent's life, so that even if they wanted to they could not stop moving forward to the inevitable conclusion.

The Chariot can sometimes represent the journey or quest itself, or it can represent the goal. The surrounding cards in the reading, or the question, will indicate this. Whether it is one or the other, it represents progress and evolution coming hurtling into the querent's life.

KEYWORDS

Progress; journey, quest; victory, triumph; evolution; promotion; conquest; contest; attainment; ambition; goal; purpose; drive; directed will; movement; momentum; focus

VIII STRENGTH

St. Perpetua
ROMAN/CHRISTIAN

The Devil has fallen dead in the dust of the Roman arena beneath the feet of St. Perpetua. The female martyr composes herself after her battle and places her hands together in prayer, casting her eyes downward as befits a wealthy Roman *matrona*, before the dust has even settled. Although she is but a young woman, Perpetua has fought an immense battle against evil and triumphed. To mark her victory, the hand of God descends, holding out a branch with golden apples upon it. Gentle woman has overcome the fierce bestial force that holds all humans (and, according to Christian belief at the time, in particular all women) back from Paradise.

As above . . .

GODDESSES AND SYMBOLS

In 203 CE, five Christians were tried and executed in Carthage for the crime of practicing Christianity. Three men—Revocatus, a slave, Saturninus, and Secundulus—were executed, alongside two women—Felicitas, a slave, and Vibia Perpetua, described as "respectably born, liberally educated, a married matron, having a father and mother and two brothers, one of whom, like herself, was a catechumen, and a son an infant at the breast. She herself was about twenty-two years of age" (quoted in Schiavo 2018, 57). Although all five Christians suffered horrific torments at the hands of the Romans, and all five died and became saints, it is Perpetua and Felicitas who are remembered from that day. Although both Felicitas and Perpetua—slave and slave owner—demonstrated immense courage and strength in their trials, it is Perpetua we see in the card image because of a vision she was granted (more on this later). What makes the account of these martyrdoms, written by Tertullian, so extraordinary is the fact that it contains testimony from Perpetua herself of her experiences leading up to her execution—one of the few examples of women's voices from this time period. It should come as no surprise to learn that Perpetua was highly literate, given that the account describes her as "liberally educated," and it appears she was fluent in both Latin and Greek.

While in prison, Perpetua reported that she had four visions. The first she interpreted as a sign that the trial of her and her fellow martyrs would end in a Passion (martyr's death) rather than freedom. In this vision she saw:

[A] golden ladder of marvellous height, reaching up even to heaven, and very narrow, so that persons could only ascend it one by one; and on the sides of the ladder was fixed every kind of iron weapon. There were there swords, lances, hooks, daggers; so that if any one went up carelessly, or not looking upwards, he would be torn to pieces and his flesh would cleave to the iron weapons. And under the ladder itself was crouching a dragon of wonderful size, who lay in wait for those who ascended, and frightened them from the ascent (in Schiavo 2018, 59).

Perpetua saw some martyrs she recognized ascending before her, and when she took the first step up the golden ladder, the dragon (or snake, a symbol of evil) raised its head as if in fear, and she trod upon its head before ascending further. By treading on the head of evil, she managed to ascend more swiftly to a beautiful garden.

In her second and third visions, Perpetua saw her younger brother, who had died as a child, in a hot place with many people who were, like him, thirsting for water and unable to reach a vast pool to quench their thirst. Perpetua, being granted spiritual strength by God, prayed for her brother and freed him from the hot place so that his soul could drink from the pool.

It was before these two visions that Perpetua and her fellow martyrs were condemned to be thrown to the wild beasts in the arena for confessing to being Christians. Due to this sentence, Perpetua's fourth and final vision before her execution continued the theme of fighting with beasts, and it is this vision that we show in the card image. In this vision, Perpetua was called out of the prison by Pomponius, a deacon who ministered to her. He led her via a long and winding road to the amphitheater, where she remembered that she was to be thrown to the wild beasts. Yet, when no beasts were let into the arena, she marveled. She further reports:

Then there came forth against me a certain Egyptian, horrible in appearance, with his backers, to fight with me. And there came to me, as my helpers and encouragers, handsome youths; and I was stripped, and became a man. Then my helpers began to rub me with oil, as is the custom for contest; and I beheld that Egyptian on the other hand rolling in the dust (in Schiavo 2018, 63).

It is clear here that Perpetua was being readied for battle and that the Egyptian she speaks of is symbolic of the devil, since she later said: "Then I awoke, and perceived that I was not to fight with beasts, but against the devil" (in Schiavo 2018, 64). The changing of Perpetua into a man is a problematic passage, and some have interpreted it to mean that in order to fight in such a battle in the arena, one had to be male. Other interpretations see this sex change as indicative of gender roles at the time. After the preparations in the vision, a man of wondrous height came forth into the arena and declared the terms of the battle: if the Egyptian overcame Perpetua (who is referred to at this point as a woman), he would kill her with the sword, but if she overcame the Egyptian, she would be given a branch with golden apples upon it as a mark of her victory. Following this, the battle commenced:

He sought to lay hold of my feet, while I struck at his face with my heels; and I was lifted up in the air, and began thus to thrust at him as if spurning the Earth. But when I saw that there was some delay I joined my hands so as to twine my fingers with one another; and I took hold upon his head, and he fell on his face, and I trod upon his head. And the people began to shout, and my backers to exult. And I drew near to the trainer and took the branch; and he kissed me, and said to me, "Daughter, peace be with you"; and I began to go gloriously to the Sanavivarian gate (in Schiavo 2018, 63).

The Sanavivarian gate was the exit from the arena in Carthage reserved solely for triumphant gladiators after gladiatorial battle. Indeed, the method of fighting used in the above passage is a mixture of a Greek martial arts contest known as *pankration* and gladiatorial combat. It is clear through this vision that Perpetua's martyrdom is a battle against the Devil, and eventually a victory against him, and it is not the last time in her trial and execution that she overcame the animalistic, bestial, and cruel aspects of human nature: she continually cowed the members of the tribune into submission with her harsh yet true words, and the crowds into submission with a single look.

When the martyrs were treated badly by the tribune and not allowed to refresh themselves in a better part of the prison for fear that they would use magic to free themselves, it was Perpetua who spoke for them:

Perpetua answered to his face and said, "Why do you not at least permit us to be refreshed, being as we are objectionable to the most noble Caesar, and having to fight on his birthday? Or is it not your glory if we are brought forward fatter on that occasion?" The tribune shuddered and blushed, and commanded that they should be kept with more humanity (in Schiavo 2018, 67).

In a similar manner, when the martyrs were brought to the arena for their execution, the tribune said they were to be dressed as pagan priests and priestesses of Saturn and Ceres, in a mockery of the martyrs. To this Perpetua protested, saying,

We have come thus far of our own accord, for this reason, that our liberty might not be restrained. For this reason we have yielded our minds, that we might not do any such thing as this: we have agreed on this with you (in Schiavo 2018, 68).

It was thus decided that the martyrs were to be allowed to remain dressed as they were, and they rejoiced as they entered the arena, Perpetua singing psalms and "already treading under foot the head of the Egyptian." She and Felicitas were stripped naked and clothed in nets before being thrown to a wild cow, but the audience was appalled to see "one young woman of delicate frame, and another with breasts still dropping from her recent childbirth," and so the female martyrs were recalled and dressed before being given to the cow again. (It is worth noting here that Felicitas, who was eight months pregnant upon entering prison, prayed for—and was granted—a premature delivery so that she might join her fellow martyrs in death.) With every wound Perpetua received, she retained her modesty and composure, covering herself up when her dress ripped away from her thigh, and asking for a hairpin that she might pin up her hair in a more becoming fashion: She did not want to appear as a mourner but as a proud Roman matron.

Finally, when the audience called for the martyr's deaths, they were lined up on the stage and stabbed with swords by gladiators. However, the youthful gladiator who struck at Perpetua was so afraid of her strength and courage that he missed, instead striking her between the ribs:

> But Perpetua, that she might taste some pain, being pierced between the ribs, cried out loudly, and she herself placed the wavering right hand of the youthful gladiator to her throat. Possibly such a woman could not have been slain unless she herself had willed it, because she was feared by the impure spirit (in Schiavo 2018, 70).

In some renderings of the martyrology, Perpetua breaks from conventional femininity by meeting the intrusive gazes of the crowd eager to watch her die, refuting them with her own intense gaze. It has been commented that her ability to stare directly into the faces of her persecutors instead of looking away, as traditional feminine demeanor dictated, signaled aggressiveness that was not part of conventional femininity (Shaw 1993, 139). The look showed courage, strength, and a refusal to be made passive by the voyeurism of her death. Indeed, Perpetua broke out of traditional feminine roles in her visions by asserting her power to the full: intervening on behalf of the dead, dealing directly with authority figures of early Christian ministry on an equal basis, and fighting in the arena in a male contest and winning. Throughout the account of her martyrdom, Perpetua demonstrated immense strength of body (she survived many tortures before being executed), mind (by convincing the tribune to treat the martyrs differently), soul (she overcame the Devil), and heart (at one point in the account, she gave strength to the other martyrs with her words and helped Felicitas during her suffering). In her vision she battled with the Devil himself and didn't just overcome evil but used it to ascend to Paradise after death.

. . . So below

DIVINATORY MEANINGS

Strength does not always refer to physical, brute strength, but more often in a reading it represents inner strength, courage, perseverance, and steadfastness. The image of the beast or beast-like figure in the card (in this case an Egyptian that Perpetua saw as a symbol of the Devil) often symbolizes the raw and animalistic nature of humankind, and its capability to commit evil or wrong acts. It is the savage side of our natures, the cruel side, and the side that often ignores the higher brain functions. There are many ways to approach this aspect of one's nature, but Strength advises that Vibia Perpetua's method will win the day in this situation.

This card suggests that it is the querent's strength of mind, will, and personality that will overcome the lower nature. It advises the querent that overcoming obstacles and adversity is most possible if they do so with gentleness, calmness, and a cool head, instead of stooping down to the level of the adversity. It warns against fighting fire with fire.

At other times, Strength can indicate that the obstacle or adversity itself can be used by the querent to rise above it: Just as Perpetua recognized the dragon at the foot of the golden ladder and used it as a step upward, so the querent can acknowledge their own bestial and lower natures and incorporate them into themselves more fully. By doing so, the querent will effectively tame the beast within, taking full control of it instead of ignoring it and allowing it one day to break free unchecked. However, the querent should guard against believing themselves completely removed from their lower natures: Within every person is the potential for cruelty, lust, jealousy, and animalistic needs. Indeed, it is only by virtue of the fact that Perpetua had a physical and mundane body that she was able to be martyred and thus attain Paradise.

Negatively aspected, Strength can reveal aggressiveness and an overreliance on physical strength, or it can suggest that the querent is the beast in the card image and not Perpetua. It can indicate that the querent has anger management issues or finds it difficult to control their animalistic nature, losing their rationality in the process.

Most importantly, however, Strength indicates victory over this aspect of the querent's nature, and the inner strength to see something through, no matter how painful or difficult it may be.

KEYWORDS

Strength; inner strength; willpower; courage; steadfastness; perseverance; overcoming the lower nature; aggressiveness; force; taming

IX THE HERMIT

Kwan Yin
CHINESE

The beautiful bodhisattva of compassion, Kwan Yin, "Hearer of Cries," descends into the underworld after taking on the burden of her executioner's bad karma upon her death. Her light of universal love and benevolence shines so brightly that all the trapped souls see her and look toward her for help, sustenance, and guidance in their hell. Where she walks, flowers bloom, butterflies take flight, and music fills the darkest regions of the Earth. In a supreme act of guidance, this Chinese savior extends her hands to the souls and guides them out of hell, freeing them from the wheel of reincarnation.

As above . . .

GODDESSES AND SYMBOLS

The figure of Kwan Yin can be found throughout China, Japan, India, and, more recently, in the West. She is an immensely popular figure who goes by many names: as Quan Shi Yin she is "hearer of cries," recounting a tradition that, as she was about to enter Heaven and be released from the world, she heard the cries of suffering from all living beings and turned back to the world, becoming a bodhisattva. She is also Kwannon or Kwannon-sama in Japan, and in India she has become the goddess Tara, who herself has many forms. In Pure Land Buddhism, she is called "the Barque of Salvation." In her early history, Kwan Yin was a male bodhisattva and emanation of the Buddha, Avalokiteśvara—a being formed from the tears of the Buddha when he wept for the suffering of mankind, and who was given the epithet Quan Shi Yin. This bodhisattva was worshipped popularly from around the first century CE but by the twelfth century had become depicted as female. The possible reasons for this are numerous and variable, but we know that, as the centuries passed, the figure of Kwan Yin became recognized as separate to Avalokiteśvara (Blofield 1988, 39–40).

The depictions of Kwan Yin are as varied as her names and stories. She is often shown holding a willow branch and small vase, representing the sweet nectar of wisdom and compassion, and her willingness to sprinkle it upon any who call upon her. She is also often shown holding a child, signifying the fact that prospective parents may pray to her to give them a child of their preferred sex or for safe delivery in childbirth. This particular image of her has caused many Western viewers to mistake her for the figure of Mary, mother of Christ:

> Another metamorphosis of Kwan-yin is represented in a female figure, holding in her arms a child. It is in reference to this image that a parallel has often been instituted between Kwan-yin and the Virgin Mary. A stranger who did not take

notice of minute peculiarities in dress, would very naturally have the idea of similarity presented to him, and mistake the child which the goddess presents to mothers praying for posterity, for the infant Savior. (Edkins 1893, 242)

Among folk depictions, Kwan Yin can be found surrounded by a seascape, standing upright and benevolent. Here she is a guardian and savior of seafarers and can be called upon by those in peril at sea. Like a lighthouse beacon, she is said to guide lost sailors home. This aspect of Kwan Yin as a savior is repeated throughout hymns and writings about her. A picture dated to 910 CE, currently residing in the Stein Collection, has a hymn to her on its back:

All things are born unstable as a lightning-flash;

In a moment they are destroyed for they have no permanency.

But the Compassionate Kuan-Yin rescues creatures of every sort;

In love how deep and tender she builds a bridge (to Salvation)!

Spending the fleeting wealth of this world, I have made her true image,

The beams of her light flashing and glinting in the splendour of a coloured painting.

My only prayer is that the dead may be born again in Paradise,

That, escaping the pain of the Three (Evil) Ways, they may mount to the Heavenly Halls (Waley 1920, 146).

In the *Lotus Sutra* it is said that if a person calls upon Kwan Yin's name in a single-minded way, she will save them from any conceivable calamity (Karcher 2001, 7). Later, regarding Kwan Yin, the *Lotus Sutra* says

O Radiance spotless and effulgent!

O night-dispelling Sun of Wisdom!

O Vanquisher of storm and flame!

Your glory fills the world! (trans. in Blofield 1988, 105)

The light of Kwan Yin, even in its smallest form, irrevocably redeems the darkness. If even the tiniest candle is lit in the dark, it is no longer dark. This ability to redeem the darkness and bring light to those lost and suffering can be seen in the many stories associated with Kwan Yin, including the one depicted in the card image of The Hermit.

The manuscript of *Hsiang Shan*, thought to be the research of the Buddhist monk Chiang Chih-ch'i (twelfth century CE), gives one of many versions of Kwan Yin's last human incarnation (though no date is given for this incarnation) as a girl named Miao Shan, the daughter of a provincial governor or king who had but three daughters. He wanted to get excellent grandsons, so he sought to marry his daughters to wealthy and powerful men of importance. The elder two daughters were happily married off, but the youngest, Miao Shan, refused to listen to any talk of marriage unless the marriage would heal three ills: the suffering caused by aging, the suffering caused by illness, and the suffering caused by death. When asked who could heal these, Miao Shan replied that a doctor could do so.

This greatly angered her father, since a doctor was not wealthy or important at all. In response to his anger, Miao Shan begged him to let her become a nun in a nearby temple rather than marrying. Her father agreed, thinking she would soon tire of the difficult tasks and strict daily routine observed by the nuns, and return home eager for marriage to a man of his choice. He visited the temple and requested that she be set to work on the hardest of chores every day to ensure this outcome. However, Miao Shan not only undertook this hard labor but seemed to enjoy it, and her father became frustrated. He brought her home and locked her away in a tower, feeding her only the vilest food and mistreating her, once again hoping she would submit to his wishes. This too was in vain, as Miao Shan spent her time in prayer and meditation.

Finally, drowning his sorrows in drink one night, Miao Shan's father demanded that his daughter be brought from her tower and executed for insulting the morals of filial piety. She was led to the spot where her executioner—weeping at his terrible task—awaited her, and knelt before him as he raised the sword to behead her. In one version of the story, a tempest arose and blinded the executioner, and a white tiger leapt up to Miao Shan and carried her away to a cave, whence she went to hell. In another version, Miao Shan saw the pain of the executioner, and as he struck the killing blow she voluntarily accepted the bad karma he would have reaped, and thus descended to hell upon her death.

However, when she descended to the infernal regions, her light and beauty were so powerful that where she walked, flowers grew, and where her hands stretched outward, butterflies soared and birds sang. All the damned souls in torment saw her beautiful visage and their hearts were lifted, and they reached out to her, crying for help and supplication. Kwan Yin, seeing their torment, went to the lord of hell, Yen Lo Wang, and compelled him to release them all. When this was done, he asked her to leave, and upon returning to Earth she traveled to Potala, where she spent the rest of her days in meditation and compassionate works, finally attaining bodhisattva status. In many versions of the legend she returned to her father and mother and converted them to Buddhism (Blofield, 1988, 69–72).

This story expresses the nature of The Hermit: the tiny light in the darkness that acts as a guide for the lost soul and our inner selves during difficult times. Here is also active compassion for other beings, which can come only through wisdom of one's own nature. This active compassion is a theme continued in the depiction of Thousand-Hand Kwan Yin. The origin of this depiction is a story in which Kwan Yin vowed never to rest until she had released all life from suffering, but when she strained to comprehend the needs of so many beings, she found her mind could not contain it all, and her head broke apart. Amitabha Buddha aided her, fashioning her broken head into eleven heads. Given the capacity to see and comprehend more, Kwan Yin then reached out her two hands to help as many beings as possible but could only help a few—her hands shattered into thousands of pieces under the strain. Amitabha Buddha aided her again and gave her 1,000 hands made from the shattered pieces, enabling her to help many more beings. This image of Kwan Yin demonstrates her active compassion and desire to save all sentient life from suffering and darkness. Her hands save and bless, grant aid and wisdom, and guide souls in the darkness. Each one is a beacon of light and hope.

. . . So below

DIVINATORY MEANINGS

The Hermit is a powerful card of wisdom and inner understanding. It is often depicted as lone figure in darkness bearing a staff and lantern, so this card is sometimes interpreted to mean loneliness or a loner. However, while the card can often have connotations of a solitary nature, it does not necessarily imply that the querent is on their own or has no friends. This lone nature simply relates to the fact that in order to gain the wisdom of The Hermit, we must listen to our own inner self, rather than following the ways of others or somebody else's path. The mystical path of The Hermit is hers alone and is not influenced by anybody else.

As such, this card can signify mysticism of all kinds, but particularly when the mysticism encourages the querent to focus within themselves and learn about their own nature. It is also a card of descent into the underworld—but not an underworld created from our vices and darkest aspects of our selves, rather an underworld of our own inner world. This inner world can seem dark and frightening at first, but this is only because it is usually untrodden ground. Once we enter within, however, shining a little light on it, we see more clearly. Like Kwan Yin descending into hell and redeeming its tormented souls, we can enter our own darkness and accept what we find there.

The Hermit can also represent the principles of active compassion toward others, but coming out of knowledge, wisdom, and experience. When we have redeemed our darkest nature, we have the inner light we need to help transform others. We can become a guiding light for those who are lost. At times, this card indicates the teaching of inner wisdom by using outer methods, of "bringing fire down from the mountain," or bringing spiritual teachings to others.

As an advisory card, The Hermit suggests that the querent is their own best teacher and advisor, and that they need to take some time out to consider the situation, shine some light on it through examination and solitude, and perhaps remain silent instead of speaking out. Negatively aspected, The Hermit suggests that not taking the advice of others at this time would be unwise for the querent, or that they may be the ones in need of help.

KEYWORDS

Bringing light to the darkness; illuminating wisdom and truth; offering aid to those lost in the darkness; solitude; finding comfort in being alone; quiet time for the self; reflection; turning inwards for answers; a guiding light; a loner or lone nature; the inner world; entering our own darkness

X THE WHEEL OF FORTUNE

The Moirae
GREEK

In a dark cavern bedecked with finely spun spider's web, the three Moirae—the Fates—weave the thread of a child's life. They apportion the number of years it is due, they stretch the thread to test its strength, and eventually they will cut the thread when time is up. Here is the implacable force of fate and destiny, but here too is the delicate balance of cycles and the weighing up of risk against certainty. Hanging from the webs above their heads are items that represent humankind's complex relationship with fate, destiny, free will, and the inevitable: the clock of time, the skull of mortality, the key of secrets, rings of commitment, and items of gambling. Surrounded by these, we—the newborn infant—are perpetually in the center of the wheel of fortune, waiting in the middle of the web of the Moirae.

As above . . .

GODDESSES AND SYMBOLS

The Greek word "Moirae" translates as "apportioners" and refers to the fact that the three Fates of Greek myth apportioned the life span and fate of each man and woman born. These goddesses are writ large in the Greek myths as implacable, all-controlling, all-seeing, and all-knowing deities far removed from the details of human life that they control. Instead, they are on the outside looking in, a part of the bigger picture, understanding the great cycles of life.

In their earliest form, it is possible that there may have been only one goddess of fate, spoken of generally by Homer as an inexorable Destiny:

> No; all we can do now is to sit at home and bewail our son from here. This must be the end that inexorable Destiny spun for him with the first thread of life when I brought him into the world (Homer, *Iliad* xxiv.209; trans. by Rieu in Homer 1950).

As three goddesses, the Moirae are called Clotho, Lachesis, and Atropos. Clotho, "the spinner," spun the thread of life with her distaff and spindle; Lachesis, "the allotter," measured the thread with her measuring tool and gave each person his or her lot in life; Atropos, "inevitable" (also called Aisa by Homer), cut the thread of each life with her shears and chose the manner and time of death. In some works (such as those of

Ovid), despite these foreboding images of the Fates, they are often imagined as spinning, showing their continual power over human life and its many cycles. Although it would seem that they should all be of the same age, some texts have Atropos as the oldest of the three and also the smallest in stature:

> Klotho and Lakhesis stood over them, and smaller than they was Atropos, no tall goddess, yet she it is who is eldest of them, and ranked high beyond the two others (Hesiod, *Theogony*, 258ff; trans. in Evelyn-White 2009).

This also shows that Atropos, representing the inevitable mortality, was given great honor and more power, perhaps, than her sisters. The Moirae were, variously, the daughters of Nyx (night), according to Hesiod (*Theogony*, 217); Zeus, according to Apollodorus and sometimes Hesiod; Ananke (Necessity), according to Plato (*Republic*, 617C); or Kaos, according to Quintus Smyrnaeus. Seneca wrote that the Moirae's decrees are immovable and inescapable, painting a bleak picture of free will:

> By fate are we driven; yield ye to fate. No anxious cares can change the threads of its inevitable spindle. Whate'er we mortals bear, whate'er we do, comes from on high; and Lachesis maintains the decrees of her distaff which by no hand may be reversed. All things move on in an appointed path, and our first day fixed our last. Those things God may not change which speed on their way, close woven with their causes. To each his established life goes on, unmovable by any prayer. To many their very fear is bane; for many have come upon their doom while shunning doom (Seneca; trans. by Miller in Seneca 2010, 980ff).

But it seems other writers felt there was room for maneuvering in this fate. The Moirae do not seem to interfere rigidly with human life but instead give conditional destiny to humankind, which humans therefore have the power to try to change. Some deities, such as Zeus, were also powerful enough to change or prevent somebody's apportioned fate. As in Homer's *Iliad*, some people become aware of the possibilities within the web of fate, loopholes left there to be taken advantage of:

> My divine Mother, Thetis of the Silver Feet, says that Destiny has left two courses open to me on my journey to the grave (Homer, *Iliad* Ix.411, trans. by Rieu in Homer 1950).

Thus, although the end decided upon by Atropos is inevitable and unstoppable, the manner in which the end is attained may have some flexibility. However, the Moirae were still depicted by many Greek writers and poets as ugly women, sometimes wearing beards, and with a stern, unflinching, uncaring countenance. In later myths they were confounded with their sisters, the Erinyes (called "the Kindly Ones" to prevent the speaker from incurring their wrath, but in truth called "the Furies"). In art the Moirae were depicted in contradiction to their literary descriptions: as maidens, albeit stern ones. They had sanctuaries in many places, including Corinth, Sparta, and

Thebes. In temple images, they were often depicted alongside Zeus, since Hesiod's genealogy for them gives them as his daughters, and he is said to be the one god who is more powerful than them. They were also said to be the ones who set down what Zeus decreed, and who sat closest to his throne:

> Moirai who sit nearest of the gods to the throne of Zeus and weave on adamantine shuttles countless and inescapable devices of counsels of all kinds. Aisa (Destiny), Klotho (Clotho) and Lakhesis (Lachesis), fair-armed daughters of Nyx (Night) (trans. in Campbell 1994, fragment 1018).

However, in some myths even Zeus could not escape the power of the Moirae:

> To the Moirai the might of Zeus must bow; and by the Immortals' purpose all these things had come to pass, or by the Moirai's ordinance (Quintus Smyrnaeus, *The Fall of Troy* 13.545ff; trans. by Way in Quintus Smyrnaeus 2011).

There is also suggestion that the Moirae did not look after humankind's lot only but also watched over the laws of nature and the heavens, ensuring that sacred laws and oaths were kept. The yearly descent and ascent of Persephone (or Proserpine) was presided over, aided, and set in stone by the Moirae, who therefore helped set the seasons in their order:

> [The Horai, Seasons] attending Proserpine, when back from night, The Fates and Graces lead her up to light; When in a band-harmonious they advance, And joyful round her, form the solemn dance (Orphic Hymn 42, to the Seasons, trans. in Taylor 1792).

In fact, the conditions for Persephone's return to Hades once a year were set down by the Moirae:

> Proserpina shall reach the sky again on one condition, that in Hell her lips have touched no food; such is the rule forestablished by the three Parcae [Moirae] (Ovid, *Metamorphoses* 5.520ff; trans. by Melville in Ovid 1986).

In a similar fashion, the wishes of the Moirae ordained more divine order in Artemis's role as helper of birthing women: Just as Artemis's mother suffered no pain at her birth, so the Moirae decreed that Artemis would appear to birthing women who called on her (Callimachus, *Hymn 3 to Artemis*, 22ff). The Moirae also assigned to the goddess Athena eternal virginity, and to their sisters, the Erinyes, the Moirae assigned the role of punishers of wickedness and bringers of justice (Aeschylus, *Eumenides* 334ff).

Perhaps one of the most beautiful descriptions of the Moirae comes from Plato:

> The Moirai, daughters of Ananke, clad in white vestments with filleted heads, Lakhesis, and Klotho, and Atropos, who sang in unison with the music of the

Seirenes (Sirens), Lakhesis singing the things that were, Klotho the things that are, and Atropos the things that are to be. And Klotho with the touch of her right hand helped to turn the outer circumference of the spindle, pausing from time to time. Atropos with her left hand in like manner helped to turn the inner circles, and Lakhesis alternately with either hand lent a hand to each (Plato, *The Republic*, 617C; trans. by Shorey in Plato 1930).

Here, Plato gives an otherworldly quality to the Moirae, granting them the ability to see the past, present, and future; they are spinning, a recurring theme throughout the mythology of the Moirae. This suggests an image of each individual human life as a golden thread and demonstrates metaphorically that just as individual threads combine to make a finished tapestry, so do individual lives unite and form a complex web that cannot be untangled. If one thread is broken, it shakes the web. This shows the connectedness of the universe and human lives. This interconnectedness, and the power of the Moirae to know all the lines and threads of the world, is shown by Ovid, who wrote that the Moirae possess, in their dwelling, a huge tapestry detailing all the threads they have spun:

Child, do you mean, by your sole self, to move unconquerable fate? You are allowed to enter the three Sisters's [Fates'] dwelling. There a giant fabric forged of steel and bronze will meet your eyes, the archives of the world, that fear no crush of heaven, no lightning's wrath, nor any cataclysm, standing safe to all eternity. And there you'll find engraved on everlasting adamant the fortunes of your line. I read them there myself and stored them in my memory and I'll declare them that you may not still labour in ignorance of things to come (Ovid, *Metamorphoses* 15.807ff; trans. by Melville in Ovid 1986).

Further, the knowledge of such larger patterns is hinted at by Plato, when he writes of the fates of the souls who go to Hades after death and are given new fates by the Moirae, suggesting that their deaths are a prelude to another life, perhaps reincarnation, and that the Moirae were mistresses of this cyclical process:

Now when they arrived they were straight-way bidden to go before Lakhesis, and then a certain prophet first marshalled them in orderly intervals, and thereupon took from the lap of Lakhesis lots and patterns of lives and went up to a lofty platform and spoke, "This is the word of Lakhesis, the maiden daughter of Ananke (Necessity), souls that live for a day, now is the beginning of another cycle of mortal generation where birth is the beacon of death" (Plato, *The Republic*, 617C, trans. by Shorey in Plato 1930).

The Moirae, givers of destiny at birth, and takers of lives at death, know and hold the power over the many cycles and processes of each individual thread and the greater threads of the tapestry of the universe. They are outside the usual realm of the gods and certainly outside the realm of humankind; it is rarely given to humans to see the threads of destiny, but instead the Moirae's unflinching dictates inspire humankind to find, among the tangled web of fate, the central point from which the processes and cycles can be faced.

. . . So below

DIVINATORY MEANINGS

In a reading, the Wheel of Fortune can be a complex card to interpret. It represents cycles and processes, in particular the process of change, which is a constant. It reminds the querent that they cannot stop changing but instead must embrace the changes that are happening around them or to them. This card is like a complex mechanism of cogs and wheels that the querent is caught up in: If they try to stay still, they will be crushed, but if they move with the flow of the mechanism, they can prevail.

This card often suggests that there are bigger things at work in the issue than the querent may be aware of, that the current issue is simply one stage in a longer process, and that things will not remain as they are for very long. Therefore, it also advises the querent not to place too much store in the present situation but instead be prepared to take risks, gamble, and let go when necessary. If the querent is undergoing a particularly stressful situation, this card suggests that it would be useful for them to find a center of gravity, placing themselves in the center of the rotating wheel, rather than wasting their time getting dizzy on the outside of the rotations.

The Wheel of Fortune often indicates issues of control or lack thereof, but the surrounding cards will indicate whether the querent needs to try to reclaim control, or if they would benefit more from letting go and being taken on a rollercoaster ride.

KEYWORDS

Change; process; cycle; chance, luck; fate, destiny; gambling; risk; fortune; choice; control

XI JUSTICE

Ma'at
EGYPTIAN

The great eyes of Ma'at oversee the universe in all its connectedness; sitting with her back to the tree made entirely of the energy that permeates the continuing creation of the world and everything in it, the later form of Ma'at as a goddess holds the symbols of life and law in each of her hands. She wears the white ostrich feather sacred to her upon her brow, just as the less anthropomorphized concept of her does, reminding us that the law here is not just human reward and punishment but also world order and the continuing balance of the universe. The many branches of the tree tell us that the reach of this law is all-encompassing, touching not only the human world but also the realm of the gods and even the dead. Over all this is the weighing of the human heart, at death, against the feather of Ma'at, the symbol of order and balance. Only if the heart is found to be in balance with the rightness of divine law can the soul pass to the afterlife.

As above . . .

GODDESSES AND SYMBOLS

Although we have included Ma'at as a goddess here, she was not always so. Many of the Egyptian records indicate that ma'at was often viewed as a concept but that because this concept was so important, it became personified as a goddess, or two goddesses (depending on the record). In some records, in fact, ma'at and Ma'at existed together; the term "ma'at" was also used as a noun to describe truth or rightness. Despite many of the textual sources referring to the concept of ma'at rather than the goddess Ma'at, we still refer to them, since they highlight the significance and meaning of later references to the goddess Ma'at. It is clear, though, that Ma'at as a goddess is a fairly early development in ancient Egyptian history, being first recorded in the Old Kingdom—between 2680 and 2190 BCE. It should also be noted that there are many different spellings for the name, including Maat, Ma'at, Maāt, and Mayet; this is due to the fact that ancient Egyptian hieroglyphics do not translate cleanly into the Latin alphabet.

The goddess Ma'at is usually depicted as a young woman holding the *was* scepter (symbol of power, a stylized animal head atop a long, straight staff with a forked end) in one hand and an ankh (symbol of life) in the other. Sometimes she is depicted with wings on each arm or as a woman with an ostrich feather on her head (Budge 1969a, 416). She is usually shown standing upon a wedge-like shape, which some have suggested to be a flute, others a cubit or, more specifically, the measure of a cubit. E. A. Budge suggested the latter because it is a form of measurement.

The word or name "ma'at" translates roughly as "that which is straight." Budge makes the point that

> it is probably the name which was given to the instrument by which the work of the handicraftsman of every kind was kept straight; as far as we can see the same ideas which were attached to the Greek word *kanon* (which first of all seems to have meant *any* straight rod used to keep things straight, then a *rule* used by masons, and finally, metaphorically, a rule, or law, or canon, by which the lives of men and their actions were kept straight and governed) belong to the Egyptian word *maat*. The Egyptians used the word in a physical and a moral sense, and thus it came to mean "right, true, truth, real, genuine, upright, righteous, just, steadfast, unalterable, etc." (Budge 1969a, 417).

This indicates that Ma'at was a concept or goddess concerning not only human justice and the judgment of what is right, but also a more cosmic, universal kind of justice in the form of world order, harmony, and balance. The ancient Egyptians believed that the world around them, in all its forms, was ordered and regular, and that chaos was the enemy; the universe was predictable and constant and it functioned perfectly, with everything having its own unique purpose. Justice in this sense is concerned with the maintenance of the balance that enables the cosmic clock to keep ticking, with all its cogs and parts whirring away to keep the greater machine moving correctly. Ma'at was therefore also the goddess who regulated the stars, the seasons, and the actions of all humans and deities, and it was she that gave order to the chaotic universe at the moment of creation. Her opposite was called Isfet ("violence/injustice"), the concept of chaos personified (Assman 2006, 34). In later Egyptian religion, goddesses were usually paired with a male deity—Ma'at was paired with Thoth, the inventor of writing and the calendar, the law-keeper, and scribe.

In myth it is said that Ma'at was the daughter of Ra, and at the creation of the universe Ra raised her from the chaotic waters to aid him in his act of creation. As such, in some records Ma'at is conflated with Tefnut, another daughter of Ra, who is the eye of Ra. Despite being the daughter of Ra, however, Ma'at's dominion even held sway over him, reminding us that order and balance must be upheld by the gods as well as humans:

> Praise be to thee, O Ra. Exalted Sekhem, Mighty One of journeyings; thou orderest thy steps by Maat (Budge 1969a, 346).

In particular, the pharaoh was the enactor and maintainer of ma'at during his reign. Pharaohs were often depicted with the various emblems of Ma'at, showing that they implemented and followed the law in both a moral and spiritual sense (McCall 1990, 46). In the *Pyramid Texts*, the pharaoh is urged to be like Re (Ra), the sun god, particularly in his relation to Ma'at:

May you shine like Re; repress wrongdoing, cause Ma'et to stand behind Re"
(Faulkner 1969; *Utterance* 586:1582–83).

Cosmic order (i.e., the Sun) is reflected in mundane order, cosmic goodness through human morality. The pharaoh had a duty to help further it, and in doing so, he became part of the cosmic order. When he achieved it, he

> ascended on a cloud, he has descended . . . Ma'et in the presence of Re on that day of the Festival of the First of the Year. The sky is at peace, the Earth is in joy, for they have heard that the King will set right [in the place of wrong] . . . the King [is vindicated (?)] in his tribunal on account of the just sentence which issued from his mouth (Faulkner 1969; Utt. 627:1774–76).

It was believed that part of the pharaoh's duty, in keeping with Ma'at, was to speak truth. In the *Pyramid Texts*, the term "ma'at," not referring to the goddess but to the concept, meant, literally, "truth." The last utterance in the text states,

> Collect what belongs to truth [ma'at], for truth [ma'at] is what the King says (Faulkner 1969; Utt. 758:2290).

Ma'at, as both goddess and concept, was so all-encompassing that she governed every possible aspect of human existence and the wider world. She was concerned with the institution of divine offerings to the gods:

> They shall have their offerings by means of the word [that becometh] Maāt; they shall have their oblations upon Earth by means of the word [that becometh] Maāt (Budge 1996, 156).

Further, by performing or taking part in religious ritual, the priest, priestess, or devotee helped maintain the order and rightness of the universe that Ma'at had set down. By giving offerings, the devotee continued walking in ma'at. As such, we often find images of a priest offering a figurine of Ma'at to a deity, indicating that rightness and order had been established by the ritual (Rundle-Clark 1991, 27). She was also clearly shown as ruling in the afterlife, showing that even death and postdeath are in the remit of order. In the New Kingdom books of the underworld, particularly the sources detailing the Amduat, we are told that:

> [I]n the middle register, the goddess Maat appears twice directly in front of the solar barque; later, she will appear at the beginning of the second hour, stressing that justice and law rule even here in the afterlife" (Hornung 1999, 34).

It is clear that the remit of Ma'at is not just justice as we might define it today. She did not govern the details of law and how it was applied during trial, reward, or punishment, but rather the spirit in which it was created and upheld. However, those who wrote down the law or gave order to the chaos of thoughts—scribes—were often called priests of Ma'at and, from the Fifth Dynasty onward, the vizier responsible for justice was also called the priest of Ma'at. In later periods, those who were judges wore images of Ma'at upon their person (Morenz 1973, 117–25).

Ma'at's most famous role in Egyptian mythology is that in which she judges the souls of all the dead in the Duat (or Amduat). In the *Book of the Dead* and in many images from ancient Egyptian tombs, we find a scene of the jackal-headed god, Anubis, overseeing the weighing of the deceased's heart against the feather of Ma'at on a set of scales. Awaiting the result is the lioness Ammit, whose role it was to devour the souls of those found unworthy. In some scenes, Osiris presides over the weighing and Anubis brings the soul to the judgment. This judging takes place in the Hall of Two Truths, or Two Ma'ats, and many texts mention a judgment being made by the Two Ma'ats. The outcome of this weighing was that if the heart was equal in weight to the feather of Ma'at, the deceased could pass from the Duat to the afterlife with the other blessed dead; however, if the heart weighed more than the feather, Ammit would devour the heart and the deceased would be condemned to remain in the Duat.

There is much misinterpretation applied to this motif. Since the Western mind sees the heart as the seat of emotion, the weighing is often seen as being symbolic of the deceased reaching death with a light heart, unburdened by regret, sadness, or wrongdoing—we have all heard of the phrase "a heavy heart." However, for the ancient Egyptians, the heart was the seat of the soul, not the emotions, and it was this soul that was immortal. The feather in this case does not represent weightlessness or a lack of burden but instead is Ma'at's most sacred symbol, representing order, the balance of the universe, cosmic law, rightness, truth, and world order. Thus, the soul at death had to be in line with the cosmic order, having lived according to the balance of the universe, having spoken what is right, having walked in the path of order, and having helped institute and maintain it. When the soul does not meet these criteria, it is punished not with retribution but with remaining stuck in the Duat. Imbalance, chaos, untruth, and nonrightness are responded to with stagnation. Only when order is achieved can change—the only constant in the universe—be experienced. Just like the fine balancing act of the scales, the balance of the universe is not static but an ever-present fine-tuning of action and reaction, call and response, creation and destruction.

Great is Mayet, lasting and penetrating, it has not been disturbed since the time of him who made it. That it should be lasting is the nature of Mayet (quoted in Rundle-Clarke 1991, 65).

... *So below*

DIVINATORY MEANINGS

The name of this card can often lead to an assumption about its meaning that doesn't always encompass its otherwise broad interpretation. When we think of justice, it is to evoke images of a court of law, legal contracts, witnesses to crime, and the system by which we punish society's wrongdoers. It might also bring to mind a more personal kind of justice, wherein we give "just deserts" to those who have personally wronged us by getting revenge or giving them a taste of their own medicine. All of these things can be found in the Justice card, but it has meanings beyond that.

Often, Justice appears in a reading to raise issues of balance and order in the querent's life. It suggests, when surrounded by positive cards, that this is a time of good balance for the querent when they can be certain that although change will occur, they will never be at a serious loss of anything. The path they are on may shift slightly, but the goal will not waver. It also brings to the table any questions about how the querent orders their life and the qualities required to organize their approach or resources. With regard to a particular project, this card advises the querent to get organized quickly and stay organized but also to be flexible in response to demands on their time, attention, and resources. Above all, if they are averse to flexibility and change, they may find themselves unable to maintain the necessary balance in order to move forward.

If this card is accompanied by negative cards, it can indicate that the querent is currently in a situation of imbalance. They may find that they are not acting according to order or what is required of them, or that they are too disorganized. This card often shows up to reassure the querent that a certain path or set of results is, despite all appearances, going the right way and is acting in accordance with an overall order and balance, so they should let it run its course. Justice also asks the querent to consider the reactions or responses that will come of their actions, and they are reminded that everything they do has consequences. No person is an island. Everything they do sends ripples out into the universe and affects others, their community, and the environment. If they act in a certain way in one area of their life, they must be aware that other areas of their life will not be untouched by it. As such, this card asks the querent to take a look at the bigger picture and weigh up how their path will affect all parts of their life.

Sometimes this card appears in a reading to point to legal matters, contracts, or protection via law, or being called to serve on a jury or give a witness statement. Criminal activity being brought to justice can sometimes be indicated, especially if Justice is accompanied by cards that suggest returns or harvest. If the querent is seeking advice, this card strongly recommends that the advice should be legal in nature.

In a reading about relationships, Justice usually indicates a well-balanced partnership that allows plenty of room for flexibility and movement, but that never loses sight of its balance and center. On a personal or spiritual level, this card asks the querent to make a decision based on what they feel is closest to truth and the balanced heart of the matter.

KEYWORDS

Balance; order, law, giving order to chaos, organization, partnership, legal matters, justice, moral order, cosmic order, cause and effect, action and reaction, weighing up

XII THE MYSTIC
(THE HANGED MAN)

St. Teresa of Ávila
HISTORICAL CHRISTIAN

Borne aloft above a sea of turbulent tears, St. Teresa of Ávila closes her eyes in rapture and pain as the red-hot golden spear of her vision is driven into her heart. Wielded by an angel sent by God, unseen in this image, the spear is a ray of divine light, God's will and grace uniting with the saint. Her hands are clenched and her wrists are together, both as if in prayer and as if bound, and she gives herself up entirely to the flow of her vision and the will of God. The visions granted to her open her inner eye to new worlds, and the concerns of this world fall away. The blessing of the suffering St. Teresa endures in her union with God feeds the ocean of tears and makes her into a mystic, contemplative, and visionary. She begs that she might give her soul up to that sweet suffering again, that she might give her will to God and be borne aloft in his grace: "Lord, either let me suffer or let me die."

As above . . .

GODDESSES AND SYMBOLS

The Mystic is a card of great contradictions and opens up a cycle of cards in the Major Arcana that journey ever inward, deeper into the spiritual matters of the soul. It is as though the card before it, Justice, was a tipping point, a waypoint, after which the foundational concerns of identity and the fundamental forces of creation, life, and nature are left behind and we concern ourselves with turning within. Unlike many of the cards that come before it in the Major Arcana, it is a card of process rather than concrete state. This process is a going down into the underworld, a descent. In this sense, it has some commonalities with the Rebirth card, although the Mystic cocoons itself within the darkness of its descent, within its silence and inwardness, in order to suspend itself or remove itself from what came before. In Rebirth, the descent simply precludes an ascent back out of that darkness, and it is certainly not a darkness that is used as a place of spiritual ecstasy. Due to its connotations with deeply spiritual themes, it can be difficult at first to apply the Mystic card to everyday readings; it is important to remember, however, that the spiritual world is a reflection of the mundane world, and every spiritual process or state can be applied on a mundane level. Here, in the Mystic, is a moment of suspension, of giving up and giving in, allowing oneself to be carried along by the flow of another's will or events. Here, sacrifices are made so that transformation and progress can occur, and suffering is but a means to an end.

As a card of spiritual suspension, turning inward, and giving oneself over to other forces, the Mystic is best represented by a spiritual mystic or visionary. St. Teresa of Ávila (1515–82) was baptized Teresa Sánchez de Cepeda y Ahumada and is also known as St. Teresa of Jesus. She was a Carmelite nun during the Counter-Reformation and worked to establish several new monasteries that followed a more contemplative way of life. The reform work she undertook aimed to create environments and codes that would allow the order to turn away from vain, material things more easily and turn instead inward toward contemplation—something St. Teresa felt unable to do in her first monastery. She was also a prominent mystic, theologian, and advocate of contemplative prayer who was followed by St. John of the Cross. Her work led to the establishment of the Discalced ("Barefoot") Carmelites, an order of men and women who devote themselves completely to contemplative life and prayer. She wrote a number of works during her lifetime, all with a focus on the contemplative life. In *The Way of Perfection*, she described the method of attaining spiritual perfection through prayer, outlining its four stages—meditation, quiet, repose of the soul, and union with God. In *The Interior Castle*, she described the soul as a diamond castle with seven mansions, each of which represented a stage in the process of the soul's union with God through contemplative prayer. Both these works were written as guides for the nuns of the Carmelite order. In her autobiography, she discussed many of the same themes but also described her own experiences and events in her life. St. Teresa was canonized in 1622 and named a Doctor of the Church in 1970, alongside St. Catherine of Sienna, the two becoming the first women to be named such.

Among her writings, St. Teresa is perhaps most well known for her description of a vision she experienced that vividly encapsulates the idea of spiritual suffering, rapture, and spiritual union with the divine. She described a beautiful angel with a countenance of flashing fire.

> In his hands I saw a long golden spear and at the end of the iron tip I seemed to see a point of fire. With this he seemed to pierce my heart several times so that it penetrated to my entrails. When he drew it out, I thought he was drawing them out with it and he left me completely afire with a great love for God. The pain was so sharp that it made me utter several moans; and so excessive was the sweetness caused me by this intense pain that one can never wish to lose it, nor will one's soul be content with anything less than God. It is not bodily pain, but spiritual, though the body has a share in it (St. Teresa of Ávila; trans. in Peers, 2002, 193).

This ecstatic suffering was a recurrent theme of St. Teresa's teachings, and she considered it a vital stage of the journey of the contemplative mystic toward union with God. In *The Interior Castle* she described the response of the soul to being called inward by God as a painful one:

> [A]t first, it trembles and complains, though it feels nothing that causes it affliction. It is conscious of having been most delectably wounded, but cannot

say how or by whom; but it is certain that this is precious and it would be glad if it were never to be healed of that wound (St. Teresa of Ávila, trans. in Zimmerman, 1911, 93).

Due to the necessity of the suffering felt during the rapture of turning inward and experiencing union with God, St. Teresa wrote that "[t]o die and to suffer must be our desires" (trans. in Peers 2002, 269). Today, the motto "Lord, either let me suffer or let me die" is associated with her, since it advocates the importance of seeking the suffering rapture of divine union.

Part of the journey of contemplation into an inner life of union with God, according to St. Teresa, is giving up control. She told the nuns of her order:

But, daughters, if you would purchase this treasure of which we are speaking, God would have you keep back nothing from Him, little or great. He will have it all (trans. in Zimmerman, 1911, 70).

In The Mystic, we are called to sacrifice by giving our all to something. St. Teresa further described how contemplative mystics are to give control to God by recalling a phrase spoken by the Bride in the Song of Songs—"The King brought me into the cellar of wine." She explained that:

She does not say she went of her own accord, although telling us how she wandered up and down seeking her Beloved. I think the prayer of union is the "cellar" in which our Lord places us when and how He chooses, but we cannot enter it through any effort of our own (trans. in Zimmerman 1911, 73).

In The Mystic of the Tarot, we must learn to give up and give in, allowing ourselves to follow the flow of something rather than pushing against it or forcing an issue. The Mystic hands over the reins of power and direction. As St. Teresa said, "I know that it can only be gained by abandoning everything" (Anderson 2006, 329).

In The Mystic, a period of suspension of activity or thought is offered. Like the hanged man that gives the original card its name and image, the individual is suspended in time, hanging in a liminal moment and state. This is also a chance to turn everything on its head, seeing things from a different perspective. St. Teresa described this state as the soul being:

fast sleep as regards the world and itself in fact; during the short time this state lasts it is deprived of all feeling whatever, being unable to think on any subject, even if it wished. No effort is needed here to suspend the thoughts: if the soul can love it knows not how, nor whom it loves, nor what it desires. In fact, it has died entirely to this world, to live more truly than ever in God" (trans. in Zimmerman 1911, 70).

It is here, suspended in a liminal state, in contemplation and silence, that we might find ourselves finally open to transformation. St. Teresa described this with the analogy of a silkworm, which remains in stasis as an egg until warm weather, then hatches and feeds off the mulberry trees when they are in leaf. The caterpillar nourishes itself until it spins a cocoon of silk "in which it buries itself." When it emerges, it has died to itself, lost its life in the process of cocooning itself in stasis once more. She explains that

> the silkworm symbolizes the soul, which begins to live when, kindled by the Holy Spirit, it commences using the ordinary aids given by God to all, and applies the remedies left by Him in His Church, such as regular confession, religious books, and sermons.... Then it comes to life and continues nourishing itself on this food and on devout meditation until it has attained full vigour. ... When the silkworm is full-grown..., it begins to spin silk and to build the house wherein it must die (trans. in Zimmerman 1911, 75–76).

The silkworm enclosing itself in a cocoon wraps itself in silence, turning completely inward, giving itself over to a primordial process over which it has no control, just as the contemplative person wraps themselves in stillness and silence. Thus, The Mystic spins the silk to create the cocoon that will prepare us for the next card: Death. When we fully internalize our transformation, holding ourselves within contemplation, turning within, willingly engaging in the underworld journey of The Mystic, we are ready to embrace the transformation of Death.

... So below

DIVINATORY MEANINGS

With The Mystic, we are given a card that can be viewed in a deeply spiritual way as well as in an everyday, mundane way. The question and the surrounding cards will indicate at what level the card should be read, but we must be aware that there is not always a dichotomy between the two. Everyday actions and events can reflect spiritual transformations and processes, especially with cards, such as The Mystic, that work on such a fundamental level of the self.

In a reading, The Mystic often calls the reading to a spiritual level or indicates an inner process of transformation beginning for the querent. This may be a time for the querent to turn inward, descend into their inner life, and turn away from a focus on the material world. Sometimes, it can suggest that the querent has been paying too much attention to the mundane world and neglecting their spiritual life, so now is the time to nourish it once more. However, to many people this can be a frightening prospect, so The Mystic can seem to represent a descent into the underworld, a journey into the depths of the soul, or a shamanic journey into a primordial part of the self.

Often, The Mystic indicates a change of perspective or view point and asks the querent to think differently about the issue, events, or people. They may need to turn things on their head, completely altering their worldview, in order to see something as it needs to be seen or take the most effective course of action. Similarly, it may be time for them to relate to themselves in a drastically different way and reconsider the personality or self they present to the external world as well as to themselves.

The Mystic can sometimes point to an initiation into a spiritual or magical tradition, a call to contemplative life, and all kinds of spiritual practice—meditation, mental prayer, shadow work, shamanic journeys, pathworking, and more.

This card might suggest that the querent needs to take some time to pause in their actions, suspend certain thoughts, and wait. A pause might allow them to reassess the situation and receive answers. It may be that they have been exerting too much control or influence on a situation, which has not allowed it to develop naturally. Perhaps the querent needs to make space for growth and development. Depending on the surrounding cards, it might be time for the querent to hand control and direction over to somebody else.

Sometimes, this card can indicate spiritual pain and suffering. It can also point to a painful process or event in the querent's life that will, in the long run, be positive and fruitful. It can also suggest an act of suffering for others, somebody willing to take on the pain and burdens of others. It might also suggest sacrifices of many different kinds.

Negatively aspected, The Mystic is a martyr who ignores their own needs in favor of those of others, often with negative consequences. It can also point to activity and thoughts that have stagnated, or a spiritual path that is no longer being nourished.

KEYWORDS

Spiritual nourishment; a mystical or spiritual journey; descent into the underworld; initiation; turning inward, contemplation and reflection; a new perspective or viewpoint; sacrifice; a martyr; ecstatic suffering; short-term pain for long-term gain

XIII DEATH

Izanami
JAPANESE

In the depths of Yomi, the dark underworld, the mythical couple who created the eight great islands of Japan are reunited beyond death. Her pale flesh giving way to decay, her hair wild and unbound, Izanami-no-Mikoto—The Female Who Invites—is illuminated by Izanagi-no-Mikoto, whose impatience to see his dead wife causes him to go against her wishes not to look upon her. Upon being faced with the truth of her death and the ghastly visage of her rotting flesh, mother now only to maggots and the eight Thunder deities, he is terrified and runs from her. Izanami chases him through Yomi, sending the warriors and fearsome female spirits of the underworld after him. Izanagi's refusal to accept death and the changes it brings forever parts him from his wife yet establishes new life at every turn.

As above . . .

GODDESSES AND SYMBOLS

The creation of the world and many of the spirits and deities of Japanese myth is attributed to a divine sibling couple, Izanami-no-Mikoto ("Female Who Invites") and Izanagi-no-Mikoto ("Male Who Invites"). According to the *Kojiki* ("Records of Ancient Matters") and *Nihon Shoki* ("Chronicles of Japan"), the two earliest extant chronicles of Japan dating to the eighth century CE, prior to their birth came the birth of fifteen other deities, who commanded them to "make, consolidate, and give birth to this drifting land" (Chamberlain 1932, 21). The two married and together created the eight great islands of Japan, more islands, and a host of deities of the natural world.

However, Izanami was fatally wounded while giving birth to Fire-Burning-Swift Male Deity. As she lay on her deathbed, more deities were born from her vomit, feces, and urine (Chamberlain 1932, 34–35). After she died, Izanagi buried her on Mount Hiba at the boundary of the Land of Idzumo and the Land of Hahaki. From his tears was born the Crying-Weeping-Female Deity (Chamberlain 1932, 36–37), and he slew the Fire-Burning-Swift Male Deity, whose spilled blood birthed more deities. When this was done, Izanagi sought to find his wife in the underworld and bring her back, so he followed her to Yomi, asking that she come back and continue their act of creation. Izanami, whom he could not see in the gloom, said she would ask the deities of Yomi if she could be released although she had already eaten of the food of that realm, but commanded Izanagi not to look upon her. When she had been in the palace of Yomi a long time, Izanagi grew impatient and made a torch from the end teeth of one of his hair combs to illuminate his way as he followed her into the palace. There he gazed upon his wife but found that "[m]aggots were swarming, and [she was] rotting," and in her different body parts dwelt eight Thunder deities (Chamberlain 1932, 42). Izanagi fled, terrified at the sight, and Izanami cried out that he had shamed her by looking upon her, immediately sending Yomo-tsu-shiko-me (Ugly Female of Yomi) to pursue him. Izanagi, still afraid, distracted her by turning his headdress into a bunch of grapes and another of his combs into bamboo shoots, which she stopped to eat. Next, Izanami sent the eight Thunder deities she had birthed in Yomi and 1,500 warriors to pursue him, but Izanagi made them cower from him by brandishing his ten-grasp saber and three peaches from the base of the Even Pass of Yomi. Finally, Izanami herself pursued Izanagi to the exit from Yomi, whereupon Izanagi blocked the way with a huge boulder. The two, now enemies forevermore, made a promise to each other: she would kill 1,000 people of his land every day, and he would cause 1,500 to be born each day. Thus, the divine couple of creation established the interplay between life and death, creation and destruction, and made way for the multitude of transitions in between.

In the Tarot pack, Death ushers in a time of change. As such, it also brings with it fear, terror, and uncertainty. Death is the greatest of unknowns for humanity, and though we all face it, we always face it alone—it is an individual journey, and we have no way of knowing if what one person experiences is the same as another. Yet, Death in the Tarot offers a lesson: to refuse to accept change, to ignore deaths of all kinds, is to refuse the natural order; it is to deny ourselves the ability to move forward. Death is a part of life, and life a part of death—one cannot exist without the other. Yet, as for Izanami, death is not the end: nothing in the world is truly destroyed, but it only changes form. The myth of Izanami and Izanagi conveys many of these themes, as well as other, starker, darker ideas of death and change.

That the two figures who created life, the eight great islands of Japan, and so many other deities are the first to be embroiled in this cycle of life and death inextricably links life with the narrative of death. It makes death a fundamental part of our lives. This is further conveyed by the fact that many of the beings they created together "correspond to what we could call personifications of the powers of nature" (Chamberlain 1932, lii). The deities that come forth from their union are the foundations of the world as we know it. Izanami and Izanagi themselves are referred to by the *Kojiki* as "the Passive and Active Essences," and that "the Two Spirits became the ancestors of all things" (Chamberlain 1932, 4). The relationship between life and death is our ancestor, our origin, and our foundation. It is from where we come and to where we shall one day return.

The story also shows the establishment of the cycle and balance between life and death: whereas Izanami shows acceptance of transition by consuming the food of Yomi, Izanagi refuses to accept his wife's change when he flees from her rotting, maggot-ridden form. In doing so, Izanagi is refusing to accept the natural way of things—no wonder she cries out, "You have shamed me!" before she gives chase.

In the Tarot, Death, as change and transition, is a generative force. From its decay, from the ashes of the old, the new is fertilized and grows. This is shown in the story of Izanami when, even while dying, the signs of her sickness—vomit, feces, urine—create deities, and when the grief of Izanagi—in his tears and his killing of the child that took its mother's life—brings forth more deities. Every act of destruction in this tale is an act of creation, just as the act of creation is Izanami's destruction. The Crying-Weeping-Female Deity being born from Izanagi's tears also shows us the productive and creative power of grief that is channeled and expressed, and of transition faced and engaged with. Throughout the period of his refusal to face his wife's death, of his fleeing from her, Izanagi's actions create no more deities—yet Izanami gives birth to eight Thunder deities even when dead. Only afterward, when Izanagi purifies himself having escaped Yomi and his rotting wife, are deities once again created from his actions and ablutions (Chamberlain 1932, 46–51). During this purification, Izanagi acknowledges what has happened and symbolically washes it away, allowing himself to move on.

Some of the more terrifying aspects of death and facing transition can be seen in the card and the tale. In nearly all cultures, death is seen as an unstoppable force that cannot be escaped. The aggressive pursuit of Izanagi by Izanami in Yomi is symbolic of death's relentless pursuit, and although Izanagi succeeds in blocking his wife's way, her reach over the inhabitants of the land of the living cannot be stopped. All Izanagi can do is create in response to her destruction, replacing the 1,000 dead by her hand each day with 1,500 new beings. This is as much fact as it is poetic imagery of life triumphant: in a world where resources are correctly distributed, harnessed, and stewarded, growth increases.

The tale also portrays death as hungry: Izanagi's creation of grapes and bamboo sprouts distracts the Ugly Female of Yomi, who pauses her pursuit to eat them. The cycle of death and rebirth is also for all, conveyed by the names of the deities—Female Who Invites and Male Who Invites. Death discriminates against nobody.

In the card image, the underworld, Yomi, is depicted as a watery place, although the original texts suggest it is a place of shadows. This choice was made to utilize the Japanese concept of elemental water, which is a fluid, flowing element linked to the formless things of the world. Water adapts to its environment, flowing in a direction presented to it. In the same way, the Death card invites us to adapt to a changing situation and shift our mode of being. It asks us to remember that it is thanks to the generative power of change that formless things are given potential and, eventually, manifestation.

Despite the ubiquity of death, change, and transition, these things hold great terror for many people. The macabre fascination with, and fears of, the spirits of the dead in many cultures shows the hold that death has over our imaginations and nightmares. In Japanese folklore, for example, the spirits of the dead are both a fact of life and something to avoid discussing (Iwasaka and Toelken 1994, 6–8). Many vengeful or melancholic female ghosts appear to the living with unbound, long, wild hair—just as Izanami does in the Death card. Her tendrils of hair become menacing, shadowy hands that reach out to grasp Izanagi. She also looms much larger than her living husband, conveying the feeling of being overwhelmed by the mighty and unstoppable force of change.

. . . So below

DIVINATORY MEANINGS

Death is a powerful, evocative card that has a vast array of possible meanings. It is one of the most abstract cards of the Major Arcana, while simultaneously being the most ubiquitous. At its most basic, the Death card indicates change and transition. This can come in many forms, from a relocation and career change to a process of spiritual or even physical death. This card ssuggests endings of all kinds, some gentle and easy, some tumultuous and painful.

In relationship questions, this card suggests the ending of a friendship or romantic relationship. Unlike The Tower, however, this ending feels natural, right. The querent may feel that the relationship has run its course and would only stagnate if it continued. The Death card rarely indicates a sudden, unexpected ending, so the querent and/or their partner(s) may have been feeling that it is time to part for a while. However, this card might also indicate a big change to the nature of the relationship, its parameters, or an approach to it. Certainly, one phase is over and a new one is available.

In readings about career, a new job is on the cards or necessary. The querent may be stagnating in their current role, underappreciated or not using their skills. Now is the time to make the change—the Death card promises it will be for the better, even though it is likely to be uncomfortably different at first.

Spiritually, Death is a powerful indicator of transformation. The process of death and rebirth is vital to any spiritual path, and one that may be experienced several times by an individual. The querent is advised to embrace this process, as terrifying as it may be, and allow themselves to be carried by the flow of transition to a new state of being, a new understanding, a new awareness, or a new sense of self.

Sometimes this card can appear in a reading to indicate physical death, often an expected, natural one. It does not promise that the death will not be painful for those left behind, of course, but offers the querent some comfort in the reminder that death is a fundamental part of our existence, and that nothing in the universe is destroyed—it just changes form. Nevertheless, when accompanied by cards that suggest sadness, Death can point to the grieving process and may suggest that the querent is stuck there and having difficulty finding their way on the new path ahead of them. Surrounding cards might give advice for them on living with their grief and accepting the death of a loved one, or their own death.

Negatively aspected, the Death card indicates absolute refusal to accept change, terror in the fact of death, and the inability to move forward after an ending. It may suggest that the querent is holding on to the past or stuck in an old mode of being.

KEYWORDS

Death; change, transition; the generative cycle of creation and destruction; gentle and natural endings; acceptance of change; spiritual transformation; the start of a new phase

XIV ALCHEMY
(TEMPERANCE)

Cerridwen
WELSH

In her kitchen, the wisewoman Cerridwen brews a magical potion using her skill, knowledge, and experience. One hand channels power into the brew, while the other is open and upraised, drawing the power down. Behind her hang the tools of everyday alchemy: cooking utensils and herbs with which to blend perfection, something greater than the sum of its parts. In the cauldron, the white and red are mixed together, stirred by Gwion Bach, the boy Cerridwen has hired for a year and a day to perform the job. In front of the cauldron, waiting to receive the blessings of the completed potion, are Cerridwen's two children, a beautiful girl and an ugly boy; Cerridwen hopes that the potion will gift her son with wisdom and poetry to compensate for his unfortunate appearance. But as the potion's completion approaches, three drops of the brew spill from the cauldron and land upon the thumb of Gwion Bach, who, feeling the pain of his thumb burning, instinctively puts it in his mouth . . .

As above . . .

GODDESSES AND SYMBOLS

The story of Cerridwen is found in the collection of Welsh medieval manuscripts called the *Mabinogion*, translated by Lady Charlotte Guest into English for the first time in the nineteenth century and collected in the well-known format of today. The eleven tales in the collection originally appeared in the *Red Book of Hergest* and the *White Book of Rhydderch*, both dating to around the fourteenth century, though some parts of the texts appear to have been preserved from even earlier texts. Thus, while it is likely that the main body of texts is Christian, there is some possibility that they retell earlier pagan myths. Cerridwen's tale is, more correctly, the tale of the bard Taliesin and how he obtained his gifts of poetry, art, and knowledge; however, without Cerridwen, Taliesin would not have been born at all.

The *Mabinogion* says that it was during the time of King Arthur that a man named Tegid Voel lived with his wife, Cerridwen, in the midst of Llyn Tegid (Bala Lake). They had an older son, Morvran, a daughter called Creirwy, and a younger son, Afagddu, who was extremely ugly. It is interesting to note the translations of the names of Cerridwen's children: Morvran roughly translates as "big crow," Afagddu means "utter darkness," and Creirwy is possibly from the Cymric word meaning "purity"; in this sense her name means "the purest." It is also possible that Morvran and Afagddu are the same figure in the earlier tellings, becoming two figures only in the later versions. Here we have a figure of darkness, described in the tale as ugly, dark, and "the most ill-favored man in the world," and his sister, described as "the fairest maiden in the world" (Guest 2000, 127). Cerridwen's children could not be more different. In the card image we see them in the bottom corner of each card, one wearing red and the other white, one blonde and the other brunette, one bearing a cup and the other a sword. Their alchemical animal companions can be seen between them—the red lion of the divine masculine become white, and the white eagle of the divine feminine become red.

Cerridwen worried that her son was so ugly that he would not be admitted to court or accepted into polite society, so she decided he must be given the gifts of art, poetry, knowledge, and wisdom. She used her knowledge of the "arts of the books of the Fferyllt" (or, more correctly, the Book of Virgil, who at the time was attributed with great knowledge of magical arts) to "boil a cauldron of Inspiration and Science" for Afagddu (Guest 2000, 127). This potion had to be stirred within the cauldron for a year and a day, and three drops from it given to Afagddu, upon which he would receive divinely inspired eloquence and knowledge of the mysteries of the future. Cerridwen set a boy named Gwion Bach to stir the cauldron, and a blind man named Morda to tend the fire beneath it. Gwion needed to continuously stir the cauldron for the whole year and a day, while Cerridwen ensured that the correct herbs were gathered at the correct time and added to the potion.

Toward the end of the allotted time, when the potion had reached its fullness, three drops of the hot liquid spilled out from the cauldron and landed on the thumb of Gwion Bach. Because of the pain, Gwion put his thumb into his mouth and thus consumed the three blessed drops of the cauldron of Inspiration and Science. As soon as he had done this, he saw the future and understood what to do: He knew that Cerridwen would be angry at what had transpired, and so he fled to his homeland. The cauldron itself burst open, since the rest of the potion that wasn't blessed was poisonous, and the poison leaked into the land.

When Cerridwen returned from her day of gathering herbs, she saw the destruction and, in anger, struck Morda on the head so hard that one of his eyeballs fell out of its socket. He told her what had happened, and she immediately gave chase to Gwion Bach. What followed was a shape-shifting chase, a motif found throughout the folklore and songs of the medieval to early modern British Isles. First, Gwion turned into a hare to run faster, but Cerridwen became a greyhound to catch up with him; seeing her gaining on him, Gwion shifted into a fish so he could escape into the river, but Cerridwen became an otter to slide through the water and catch him, so Gwion leapt out of the river and became a bird, flying away, but Cerridwen changed into a hawk so that she could chase him across the sky as well. Finally, Gwion saw a heap of winnowed wheat in a barn, and he fell from the sky, changing into a grain of wheat. But Cerridwen shifted into a black hen, and she scratched at the grains and pecked at them until she found Gwion, whereupon she ate him.

This was not the end of Gwion Bach, however, though it may have been his death. Cerridwen became pregnant, and nine months later she gave birth to a baby boy whose countenance shone brightly. She could not bring herself to kill the child, though she knew that it was Gwion in his newest form, so instead she put him in a bag and set him adrift upon the lake, where the next day he reached the weir of a man named Elphin, who pulled the baby from the water and beheld his shining brow (a symbol of great wisdom and divine inspiration). Elphin named the boy Taliesin ("radiant brow"), and he went on to become one of the greatest bards who ever lived.

This magical story is one of the precision of alchemical transformation and of the process of mingling and balance, tempering and testing, stretching and mixing that must ensue within the "cauldron" in order to produce the necessary results. The cauldron in this tale is not only the Cauldron of Cerridwen itself, wherein the potion of inspiration is brewed, but also the womb of Cerridwen, wherein the four children of the story are all created and gestated. A range of states must be entered into at varying stages of the process, and eventually the outcome will be one that is greater than the sum of its parts. In the tale, the son and daughter of Cerridwen represent opposites: male and female, dark and light, beautiful and ugly. Taliesin, being born after them and being both the physical and magical/spiritual child of Cerridwen, is the container and unifier of these opposite states. Alchemically, the first two children of Cerridwen, Afagddu and Creirwy, can be seen as representing two different stages of the alchemical process of creating the Philosopher's Stone: Afagddu, the "utter darkness," who is possibly also Morvran, "big crow," is the nigredo (blackening) stage often depicted as a skeleton holding a black raven; Creirwy, "the purest," is the albedo (whitening) stage. Taliesin is the Philosopher's Stone attained at the end of the alchemical process, and a state of wholeness that can reached only by mingling the many and varied possibilities within.

. . . So below

DIVINATORY MEANINGS

Alchemy is a card of the process in which two opposing forces, ideas, or states are brought together—not in conflict or opposition, but in unity and synthesis. What one state lacks, the other provides, and therefore their union creates something that is far greater than the sum of its parts. But a careful balance must be sought between the two (or many—opposition and differences don't always come in pairs), not necessarily giving equal weight to both, but rather using them to their greatest efficiency. Sometimes this requires a process of eclecticism, taking bits from here and pieces from there, much like collage art. Sometimes it requires a process more like inspiration, in which two very different states, ideas, or forces inspire something that is the best of both.

When this card appears in a reading, it advises the querent that they may need to seek their solution in between two very different things, or create something new rather than following one path or another. It often suggests that the querent must seek an antithesis to their thesis, some sort of opposition to test their current path, in order to improve or progress. Alchemy is also a card of great art, work, or dreams that blaze trails rather than following old, established ways.

Often, Alchemy shows up in a reading to tell the querent that they have reached a point in their path where the results of their efforts are about to come to fruition. If this is a reading about a project or path, Alchemy is truly a blessing: it denotes not just any old work or art, but rather Work or Art that could change everything. At times this card can also refer to the process by which the querent is shaped, molded, and tempered so that their "base metal" self is transformed into their "gold" self, filled with greater potential. This process is often a difficult one, as if the querent is being forged in fire and hammered into shape. Alchemy assures them that after this difficult time, they will have gained new experiences and a greater understanding, which they can apply to new projects, ideas, or goals.

On a very mundane level, Alchemy can appear in a reading to indicate everyday acts of alchemy, such as cooking. It may ask the querent to consider taking up this art or improving it, and may point to the need for them to review their eating and cooking habits.

Negatively aspected, this card can point to something being wrong in the mix of the querent's life—it may be time for them to try to identify what the missing ingredients are, or what is making things taste so sour.

KEYWORDS

Alchemy; synthesis; transformation; eclectic; inspiration; mingling, mixing; opposites; greater than the sum of its parts; creation

XV THE DEVIL

Salome
BIBLICAL

In her stepfather Herod's feast hall, while he and her mother Herodias watch, Salome dances. Her body gyrates seductively as Herod reclines in luxury, his eyes watching and his mind imagining. Salome performs the Dance of the Seven Veils, and all that remains to cover her modesty is a thin red veil, dangerously close to falling away. In return for the pleasure her dance has given Herod, her mother demands the head of John the Baptist on a silver plate—a manipulative request that relegates Salome to the part of mere pawn in Herodias's plans. As the head of John the Baptist is brought in, still dripping with blood, Salome kisses his cold lips.

As above . . .

GODDESSES AND SYMBOLS

The Devil is a card well known to most readers before they pick up a Tarot deck, and for the notoriousness of this figure we have retained its traditional name. Yet, the image is not that of a horned goat-legged figure of evil, but instead of a young woman dancing. This is Salome, the girl known for the Dance of the Seven Veils, and it is not only her original story (although we shall see that it may not be her story at all) but also the development of her characterization over the centuries that conveys the meaning of this card.

In this card, all the ties that bind are found. Every commitment, every manipulation, every oath and bond we forge is found in the hands of the Devil, who holds those chains tightly. In some ways it is a card of being trapped, seeking liberation but being unable to achieve it. It is also an acknowledgment and acceptance of the "inner demons" of the self—the traits, desires, fears, and hopes that society deems to be unsavory, dark, or wrong. The Devil card is the home of vice and all manner of temptations. It is also a card of manipulation and power over others, often used to self-serving ends.

The Salome that we know today—the young, voluptuous dancing girl desired by her stepfather and in love with John the Baptist—is a late creation of a number of artists, writers, dancers, filmmakers, and musicians. But the earliest mention of the story in which she would eventually star is found in the Bible. In Matthew 14:6–11, we read this:

On Herod's birthday the daughter of Herodias danced for the guests and pleased Herod so much that he promised with an oath to give her whatever she asked. Prompted by her mother, she said, "Give me here on a platter the head of John the Baptist." The king was distressed, but because of his oaths and his dinner guests, he ordered that her request be granted and had John beheaded in the prison. His head was brought in on a platter and given to the girl, who carried it to her mother. (NIV)

Mark 6:21–29 has a very similar version of the tale. Although the girl in both tales is not mentioned, the name "Salome" is given as a stepdaughter of Herod Antipas in Josephus's *Jewish Antiquities* (VIII, 5:4), from the first century CE. The Salome in Josephus's work had an unremarkable life. Her second husband was Aristobulus, the king of Armenia, and as such her portrait was etched on the Armenian coins of the period (Neginsky 2013, 9). For what reason, given the historical Salome's contented and unremarkable life, would the stories attribute to her and her mother the nasty and sordid death of John the Baptist? It could be that Herod and Herodias ordered the death of John the Baptist due to the Baptist's condemnation of their marriage and his influence on the people—his condemnation of Herod could have led to open revolt. Embroiling Herodias's daughter in their plan without her knowledge could have diffused responsibility from Herod. However, it is more likely that since the Gospels were a form of ancient novel that used stylistic devices and graphic inventions to convey their message:

The evangelists consciously aspired to relieve the Roman representative—in this case, Herod Antipas—of any responsibility for the Baptist's death, just as they later exculpated Pilate. . . . It was convenient, since . . . women were depicted as devious and debauched (Neginsky 2013, 17).

In The Devil of the Tarot, a scapegoat is often required in order to establish the "moral" of a story. In this card, we find that the truth is often obscured for the sake of meaning and purpose, though this may sometimes be done for what the deceiver believes to be a good purpose. It is perhaps apt to consider that various ancient Jewish books characterized women as deceitful and cunning or as more susceptible to promiscuity than men, though also allowing that they were more fragile and weak hearted than men (Neginsky 2013, 12). It was such beliefs about the innate qualities of women that influenced laws limiting and controlling the behavior of women, both in public and in the home—an example of The Devil card's bonds created through a desire to control.

Because of its desire to control and manipulate, The Devil frequently asks us to examine the balance of power in a situation. Somebody being given the blame or assigned the responsibility for something may have little or no power, and it is often those with the least power who are most vulnerable to being manipulated by others. In the story from the gospels of Matthew and Mark, Herod was manipulated by Salome, who was manipulated by her mother, showing how The Devil sometimes indicates being manipulated by others so that you don't get what you desire but what they desire. In this card, your own desires, needs, and hopes are overlooked in favor of theirs, and you are seen as a mere pawn in their machinations. However, being powerless or lacking power can also be brought on yourself, just as Herod felt powerless to go back on what he had willingly vowed (to give his stepdaughter anything she wanted). Our inability or unwillingness to break a vow, promise, or oath can be a positive thing—such as marriage vows, business contracts, promises of friendship, or spiritual vows—but The Devil reminds us that we must therefore be cautious with what we commit to. Finally, this card asks us to consider the political, social, economic, etc. ties that bind us and influence (or force) our actions and situations.

Testament to the power of the scapegoating, manipulation, cycle of blame, and removal of power in The Devil is the tenacity of the story of Salome, who, by the medieval period, had become firmly connected with John the Baptist's death and was depicted as the personification of the lascivious woman, whose lust and desire could bring to ruin even the most holy of prophets (Barr 2008, 73). This medieval view was informed by the Church Fathers of Late Antiquity, who focused on Salome's dance and increasingly characterized it as immoral, indecent, provocative, and erotic (Neginsky 2013, 24). Herein lies another meaning of The Devil that is very much alive in the modern world: that far too often, the sexuality of women is used as the excuse for their victimization and a reason for them to be controlled. However, the power of The Devil is not gendered or targeting one gender over another—as Carter says:

> [t]he significance of the femme fatale lies not in her gender but in her freedom (Carter 1997, 251).

As the quintessential card of oppression and control, The Devil is almost malicious in its targeting of those who are liberated.

Rarely in the numerous depictions and retellings of Salome's story—and certainly not before the twentieth century—do we find Salome given the opportunity to define herself. Instead, she is defined by those around her, who place upon her their fears, desires, hopes, and machinations:

> Salome's story is a fascinating blend of Roman gossip told in cautionary tales by Seneca, Livy, Cicero, and Plutarch, New Testament Gospel, medieval legend, and Oriental Romanticism, all based on a dash of actual truth. As a creature of legend she has never been herself but always in bondage, serving men's ideas, desires, and fears about the erotic woman (Bentley 2002, 19).

In the same way, The Devil represents a situation in which we are not the protagonists of our story but the victims, controlled and limited by others. Oscar Wilde's 1893 retelling of the story, *Salome*, turns this dynamic on its head, however. In this play, it is her dance for her lustful stepfather that awakens the teenage Salome to the power of her own beauty and what it can obtain: her revenge against John the Baptist for spurning her love. This version of Salome makes a conscious choice to use her power over others to get what she wants, becoming self-directed and self-willed at the expense of others. She desires not only the death of John the Baptist as revenge but to possess him, and wantonly kisses his decapitated head before being killed by her stepfather's guards. Sometimes, The Devil shows us the power we have over others and highlights the ways in which we control or limit others. Further, Wilde's play "suggests that a striptease earned the murder of a man of God, the man who baptized Christ himself, by a man, a king, who is ruled by his flesh, not his faith. It is the triumph of sex over spirit, of pagan over Christian, of profane over sacred" (Bentley 2002, 30); this highlights the role of The Devil in the Tarot as matter triumphing over spirit, of the entrapment and limitation of spirit within manifestation.

Salome's story as it was told in later interpretations is one of obsession—obsession with John the Baptist, a man she had fallen in love with at first sight. In The Devil we find our many obsessions, all our vices and the things to which we cleave and bind ourselves. This card asks us what liberty we risk with our obsessions.

Salome was seen by later commentators in explicitly erotic terms of temptation and dangerous seduction:

> She had become, as it were, the symbolic incarnation of undying Lust, the Goddess of immortal Hysteria, the accursed Beauty exalted above all other beauties by the catalepsy that hardens the flesh and steels her muscles, the monstrous Beast, indifferent, irresponsible, insensible, poisoning... everything that approaches her, everything that sees her, everything that she touches (Huysmans 1975, 68).

It was this Salome's overt and embodied sexuality and sensuality that created vice—once again, being blamed for the responses of others.

... So below

DIVINATORY MEANINGS

In a reading, The Devil is often an unwelcome card, sometimes incorrectly so, depending on how it is aspected and on the context of the reading. Most commonly, it appears to signify commitments, bonds, promises, and vows. This may relate to contracts, such as housing contracts or contracts for a loan or credit. It may also point to contracts for a new job. Sometimes it can indicate marriage or civil partnership, and the legal, emotional, and spiritual contract the individuals make with each other. Broadly, The Devil appears in a reading to signify what ties us down, holds us down or back, and what bonds we have to each other, our situation, and the world around us. This can be seen positively in that our ties are also often our support and bonds that we have willingly chosen, but it can sometimes be negative in that at times we may feel trapped or forced into a situation by various influences or people.

Spiritually, The Devil represents the settlement of spirit in matter, its descent into the mundane world. Instead of an ascent of the soul toward a "higher" consciousness or light, the querent's spirit may be yearning for manifestation in the everyday world or may need to explore the darkness of itself in all its truth, both good and bad, vice and virtue. The Devil challenges the spiritual seeker to face themselves fully and discount nothing, barefacedly accepting even the worst parts of themselves. This card reminds the querent that to deny or ignore their vices, inner demons, or fears will result in poor spiritual health and an ignorance of the truth of their self. Sometimes The Devil can also point to various aspects of the querent's sexuality, their acceptance and understanding of their body, and learning how to enjoy their sex life. Further, it can appear in a reading to point to the querent's inner fears, hopes, and desires that they wish to keep hidden and secret from others.

Sometimes this card can point to manipulation in all its forms. This manipulation may be as small as a barely considered offer that includes something to sweeten a deal that the querent may otherwise not take, or it could be as great as a concerted and conscious effort to mislead, misdirect, and have power over somebody so that they have no choice but to do your bidding. The Devil often points to a situation in which there is a power imbalance, where one individual is seeking to gain what they desire through using others as means to an end—they do not care about what the other individuals want.

Negatively aspected, this card points to an unwanted situation from which the querent feels they cannot escape. Surrounding cards may offer suggestions for liberation. It can also signify acts of scapegoating—perhaps the querent is being made to take the blame for something—or somebody using their power over a vulnerable individual to manipulate them. At its most negative, The Devil can point to extremely unhealthy relationships, where manipulation, guilt trips, gaslighting, and emotional or physical abuse occur. It is worth examining surrounding cards for suggestion of such abuse and, if the issue is raised by the querent, offering them the details of organizations that can help.

KEYWORDS

Manipulation; bonds and the ties that bind; contracts, promises, vows, and oaths; inner demons; inner fears, desires and hopes that are kept secret; inescapable situations; being forced or coerced; unhealthy relationships; spirit descending into matter; vices; sexuality and sex life; scapegoating; power over others being abused

XVI THE TOWER

Oya
YORUBA

The silence of the barren graveyard is shattered by the sudden crash of thunder and forked lightning tearing a gaping red wound in the sky. The beautifully carved tombstone—the final and long-lasting representation of the ego and the self—is struck by the jagged point of the lightning, causing it to crumble and crack all the way to the base and below. This is no ordinary storm: This is Oya, Yoruba goddess of death and destruction. When she slashes with her sacred machete, the fabric of reality is torn asunder; when she dances, she brings earthquakes and death; when she flicks her tongue, lightning darts from her mouth. She is the hurricane, sudden sweeping change and destruction, and you never see her face.

As above . . .

GODDESSES AND SYMBOLS

In Yoruba religion and mythology, the natural forces of tornadoes, hurricanes, earthquakes, and storms are the dances and movements of the goddess Oya. These natural disasters, while bringing destruction in their wake, are often viewed as a necessary agent of purification and as prevention against stagnation; hence why—in an Ifa (Yoruba divination) commentary—the messenger god Orunmila says of the tornado Oya that is sweeping through an apprentice diviner's house:

It is very white! A clean sweep!

Ifa, I say! Let her rip! *Hai!* (Gleason 1987, 39)

In all her many guises, Oya is usually—if not uniformly—viewed as a violent, temperamental, destructive force in the universe, but one that is necessary and unavoidable. She is the goddess of death, because one of the ultimate destructions of the self is physical death. She is the air and wind around us, and thus she is not only the first breath we take but also the last. Oya brings sudden change into the lives of all beings, and with it the message that if we accept and ride the winds of sudden change—if we dance on the shifting carpet and bend in the gale—we will not break but will instead evolve and grow. Thus, in the Ifa commentary above, Oya wrecks the house of the apprentice diviner but, having done so, bequeaths upon him many riches:

What wrecks your house also makes it thrive! (Gleason 1987, 42).

She is also the favorite wife, among three, of the Yoruba god of battle and thunder, Shango (Lele 2000, 395). Together they are said to ride into battle, and many often comment that Oya gives Shango the fire to fight and be triumphant. However, Oya has had another husband: Ogun, another god of battle, but also of fire and metalwork. From him she stole sacred metal weaponry, kept the machete for herself, and gave the rest to Shango.

Even the name of this goddess bears testament to her nature: "ọ-ya" means "she tore" in Yoruba. This name conveys the utter violence with which she carries out the processes of change, indicating that the change found in The Tower is not a peaceful, passive, or welcome one: Often it is dreaded, taking us by surprise, uprooting us from our comfort zones and making us vulnerable. This kind of change takes away from us all we thought was stable, and leaves us utterly shaken and without foundation. In the same way, Oya's sacred weapon, the machete, violently clears thick jungle growth, symbolically stripping away the extraneous embellishments from life. Where there are lies and deceit, Oya's sharp machete and winds tear away the veil of deception to reveal the (sometimes painful) truth. It is said of her that "with her thumbs [she] tears out the intestines of the liar" (Gleason 1987, 2).

Storms in Yoruba religion are often associated with the process of death: They are believed to mark the transition from life to death as the soul moves from this world to Oya's island (also known as Guinea) in the middle of the Niger River. Similarly, when somebody in a Yoruba community dies, their passing is heralded with the destruction of everything tied to their physical life, leaving a mess akin to that left behind in the wake of a storm. The dead person's sacred objects are smashed, jewelry is broken, and in some parts of Africa the house is pulled down over the remains (Gleason 1987, 29). Here, the things left behind that represent the dead person's self and ego are ritually destroyed, and their spirit is guided through its transition by Oya herself.

Oya has a number of names and epithets, all revealing one of her different aspects. As Yansa (or Iansa, Iansan, Yansan, and many more variations, depending on location and dialect), her name means "Mother of Nine," indicating her role as the Niger River, which is "mother" to nine tributaries. As Ọya-e-ríí-ríí she is "Oya so charming that you can't take your eyes off her," suggesting the fascination and simultaneous repulsion we feel when faced with this sort of destructive change. Egungun-Oya refers specifically to Oya as mother of the dead, and Oya-Ajere is "Oya, carrier of the container of fire." This last refers to a myth about Oya and Shango. This myth says that originally these two were not Orisha (gods, or spirits) but humans, a king and his queen. Shango found it difficult retaining his power when so many other kings ruled the land around him, so when he heard that the King of Bariba possessed a special formula that—when placed under the tongue—enabled the user to spit lightning as an offensive weapon, he craved it. He sent his favorite wife, Oya, to the King of Bariba to request some of the formula, and sure enough she got what she wanted. The myth, however, tells that she kept some of the magic for herself, giving her the power to spit lightning and destroy what she willed. Shango himself used the lightning frivolously and accidentally misdirected a bolt at his own people, whom he had vowed to protect, killing all but a few. Distraught at his action, he hanged himself from a tree but did not die. Instead, he ascended to the skies and became an Orisha. Oya, who had followed him and discovered his body, wept over her dead husband. In her grief, she descended into swampland and also became an Orisha, ruling the skies, thunder, and lightning alongside her husband as his equal.

This story emphasizes the flippant manner in which the catastrophic events of the Tower can occur. When they happen, they seem to have no purpose or reason, and to us they may seem cruel and pointless. Yet, just as Oya and Shango's grief and catastrophe started them on the path to the status of Orisha, so the destruction and unexpected disasters in our lives can be overcome and turned to our advantage. This doesn't negate the pain they will cause us—but it does make the pain a little more worthwhile.

Another myth (found in the Ifa commentaries) about Oya concerns the association of the female buffalo as her sacred animal. In this myth, Oya was a female buffalo that could shed its skin to become a woman. The woman-Oya would hide the skin in an anthill and then pick up her wares to sell them at the nearby market. However, one day a hunter spotted her doing this, and he used the knowledge to trick Oya into becoming his wife. She agreed to the marriage on one term: that her cowives were never told about her origin as a buffalo. Thus, the marriage lasted many years, and the couple had many children. But throughout the years the cowives distrusted Oya and wanted to know where she had come from and why their husband was so closed when it came to discussing her. One night, after their patience had run out, the cowives plied their husband with alcohol until he told them where he had found Oya: a fact that the wives subsequently used to verbally abuse Oya. But the wives also told Oya where their husband had been hiding her buffalo skin all these years, so Oya immediately retrieved it and put it on, turning into a magnificent female buffalo once more. She was so angry at her husband's betrayal that she rampaged through his house, destroying all his possessions and food stores and trampling his wives to death. She destroyed every part of her husband's life, leaving only her children and the man himself alive, before disappearing from their sight (Gleason 1987, 187–93).

In this myth, we see that although we do not expect the disasters that occur in our lives, they are often caused by our own actions or inactions. This is not a statement of morality but of consequences in The Tower.

Even though this card can seem negative, it also carries a positive message about destruction preventing stagnation. The experiences of this card—and of Oya—often serve to sweep away the false foundations upon which we have built our lives. Perhaps it is this aspect of Oya (who was called "swept clean" by Orunmila) that finds resonance with the female saint with which she is associated in the religion of Santeria: St. Teresa of Ávila (see "The Mystic"). The traditional image of St. Teresa shows her with a book and a sharp weapon piercing her heart, and her motto was "Let me suffer, or let me die." Although destruction and chaos always cause suffering and pain in our lives, if we don't let ourselves suffer through it we eventually stagnate in the old ruins of our lives.

In modern worship, Oya's sacred colors are maroon, brown, orange, dark red, and other earthy, burned colors. She is depicted wearing rainbow skirts to signify her links to stormy and changeable weather, and she always wears a mask.

. . . So below

DIVINATORY MEANINGS

Death and The Tower are often considered to be very similar, yet whereas Death is natural change and transition, The Tower is utter chaos and painful destruction. In a reading, this card indicates that disaster is about to strike in the most unexpected of ways. It will shock and shake the querent to their core, and they won't be the same when the storm has passed.

Often, this card points to a complete breakdown in an area of the querent's life: the breakdown of a marriage or home situation, a mental breakdown, a sudden collapse of spiritual or religious belief, the destruction of faith, sudden events causing emotional crisis, or failure. Mostly, the things that collapse or are destroyed are based on shaky or false foundations, and the shake-up serves to leave a clean slate upon which the querent can build afterward. Where there is falsehood, The Tower reveals the truth, and where there are unnecessary embellishments, this card cuts them off entirely.

The Tower can be viewed as the ego being destroyed by events or concerted effort. It can be the final straw that breaks the camel's back in a personality shift or crisis, leaving the querent's idea of self shattered and destroyed. It can also represent the querent's entire reality being torn asunder.

Usually, when this card appears in a reading, it indicates that while the querent may be aware of the events approaching or understand why they are happening at the time, the events are so chaotic that the querent is powerless to stop them. All they can do is ride out the storm and decide how to react to them. The Tower also reminds the querent that change and destruction occur all the time, and that when Oya dances into our lives we can either hide and refuse to acknowledge her, remaining solid and immovable, or we can dance with her and shift or bend with the hurricane. The one who remains immovable will simply break, while the one who bends and dances on the shifting carpet will survive—though they may take on a very different shape in the process.

KEYWORDS

Destruction; change; pain; chaos; disaster; stormy times; endings; destruction of the ego; crisis; suddenness; breakdown; suffering; catastrophe; a shake-up

XVII THE STAR

Ushas
VEDIC HINDU

In the golden sunrise of a new day, Ushas, the Vedic Hindu goddess of dawn, dances her way across the sky. Her skirts and veil sweep yellows, pinks, and blues across the stars, and her hair becomes the sun-tinted clouds. From her heart a shining light emanates, dissipating the darkness of night and illuminating the beauty of the world for all of humankind to see. Under her wondrous gaze, humans awaken; in her name, holy men begin their first religious acts of the day; with her blessing, householders draw the first milk from their cattle. In her light, hope dawns in the soul.

As above . . .

GODDESSES AND SYMBOLS

In Vedic Hindu religion, the dawn was personified as a young, maiden-like goddess who danced or rode in her chariot across the sky every morning, dispelling darkness and bringing new light to the world. Called Ushas, she also represented the power of dawn to renew the world, to bring hope and prosperity to humankind, and to enlighten the souls and minds of all. Because she was born anew every day, Ushas was called ever young and was said to give the life and energy back to the Earth just as her own energy was rejuvenated:

> Through years and years thou hast lived on, and yet
> Thou'rt ever young. Thou art the breath and life
> Of all that breathes and lives, awaking day by day
> Myriads of prostrate sleepers, as from death,
> Causing the birds to flutter in their nests,
> And rousing men to ply with busy feet
> Their daily duties and appointed tasks,
> Toiling for wealth, or pleasure, or renown (Wilkins 1900, 48).

She is praised in the *Atharvaveda*, the *Grihya Sutras*, the *Rig Veda*, and other early Hindu texts. The authors of these Vedic hymns to Ushas spoke as people who had woken from a frightful night terror, or who had toiled through the darkness to reach the forgiving and peace-bringing light. Their hymns greeting the white-robed, crimson-fingered, newborn lustered dawn are those of greeting every new day with enthusiasm, refreshment, and hope. With every prayer to the morning's light, the praises of the author ring out with wishes for a prosperous and fortuitous day, for longevity, a happy family, and many cattle. The authors of the *Rig Veda* did not wish upon the first star they saw at night, but rather on the star of morning they saw upon waking:

O Dawn enriched with ample wealth, bestow on us the wondrous gift
Wherewith we may support children and children's sons.
Thou radiant mover of sweet sounds, with wealth of horses and of kine
Shine thou on us this day, O Dawn auspiciously.
O Dawn enriched with holy rites, yoke to thy car thy purple steeds,
And then bring thou unto us all felicities (*Rig Veda*, Book 1, Hymn XCII, 13–15, trans. in Griffith 1896).

In the *Rig Veda*, Ushas is described as a beautiful young woman who has been dressed by her mother so that all may see her adornments and splendor, yet she is also lovelier than the dawn that has gone before her:

In pride of beauty like a maid thou goest, O Goddess, to the God who longs to win thee,
And smiling youthful, as thou shinest brightly, before him thou discoverest thy bosom.
Fair as a bride embellished by her mother thou showest forth thy form that all may see it.
Blessed art thou O Dawn. Shine yet more widely. No other Dawns have reached what thou attainest (*Rig Veda*, Book 1, Hymn CXXIII, 10–11, trans. in Griffith 1896).

Her youth is everlasting, as she is renewed each morning when she uncovers herself from the darkness bought about by her sister each night, yet she is also most ancient, and with every new day Ushas brings further age to every human being:

Ancient of days, again born newly, decking her beauty with the self-same raiment. The goddess wastes away the life of mortals, like a skilled hunter cutting birds into pieces (*Rig Veda*, Book 1, Hymn XCII, 10, trans. in Griffith 1896).

Yet, this march of time that brings about slow aging and death is welcomed by the hymn singer, as each day he gets older he also becomes wiser and gets to see the beauty of Ushas riding across the sky on her purple and red horses, bringing gold and treasures with her. Further, when Ushas rides triumphant across the sky, parting the way of night, she exposes the Earth and all its creatures for humankind to see, drives away demons and monsters, and lightens the vision of humans:

> Red are the kine and luminous that bear her the Blessed One who spreadeth through the distance. The foes she chaseth like a valiant archer, like a swift warrior she repelleth darkness (*Rig Veda*, Book 6, Hymn LXIV, 3, trans. in Griffith 1896).

> Dawn hath made all the universe apparent. I see the paths which Gods are wont to travel, innocuous paths made ready by the Vasus. Eastward the flag of Dawn hath been uplifted; she hath come hither o'er the tops of houses. Great is, in truth, the number of the Mornings which were aforetime at the Sun's uprising (*Rig Veda*, Book 7, Hymn LXXVI, 1–3, trans. in Griffith 1896).

When Ushas dispels the darkness, she does so not by removing the night but by revealing the treasures that have been held secret within it. In this case, the individual stars in the night sky are treasures of light, promises of hope that can be brought to the forefront if needed. The light of Ushas cannot be brought to the world without the light of the sun, and thus she is often described as the wife of the Sun and paired with the fire god, Agni.

When Ushas wakes humans from their sleep, she wakes first the priests, poets, and hymn singers, so that they may kindle the Agnihotra fires and thereby (in Hindu philosophy) re-create the world anew by ritually reenacting, in the Agnihotra ritual, the first sacrifice made by Prajapati, which initiated the genesis of creation. Thus, Ushas the dawn bringer, Daughter of the Universe, not only renews herself but also the hope of mankind and the life of the world.

... *So below*

DIVINATORY MEANINGS

The Star is a blessing in any reading; when it appears there is little that can make it negative or badly aspected. This card reminds us—often when we are at our wit's end—that hope can triumph even in the darkest times, and that there is light in the darkness, even if it is only a tiny pinprick in the night sky.

In a reading, The Star suggests that guidance is coming the querent's way in some form—maybe from another person, such as in counseling or therapy, a guidebook, a teacher—or in a sign from the universe. In this form, The Star also reminds the querent to be on the lookout for signs and signals that they are moving in the right direction, such as happy coincidences and synchronicities that make the way easier.

Often, this card appears in a reading to tell the querent that illumination or truth will soon be revealed out of confusion, and reminds the querent that sometimes we must engage with the darkness before we can see the light. It also indicates self-renewal and advises the querent to allow themselves to be refreshed and renewed after hard work or having completed a goal or met a deadline. This card points to a time of healing, rejuvenation, and self-reflection; it also points to optimism and idealism and advises the querent that wishing and dreaming is a healthy pastime and can only lead them to greater heights.

The Star advises the querent to be aspirational and to make plans to achieve their dreams, even if they think they are impossible. It may be time for the querent to take up new habits or practices that encourage and aid their aspirations, such as keeping a diary or bullet journal, making their everyday arrangements goal-driven, and assessing what they wish to achieve. It also reminds the querent to bring beauty into their everyday world and try to assess how what they do each day feeds into their greater goals and plans. It asks them to be honest about what positively contributes to their dreams and what holds them back.

If this card appears in a reading about a possible new project, relationship, goal, or plan, it suggests that the querent should throw themselves wholeheartedly in, as they will see great things and find it extremely rewarding. If it appears in a reading about something the querent is hoping and wishing for, it offers a positive response but reminds them that wishing is just the beginning of greatness.

KEYWORDS

Enlightenment; renewal; healing; rejuvenation; illumination; optimism; dreams, wishes; goals; fame; guidance; hope

XVIII THE MOON

Morgan la Fey
MEDIEVAL BRITISH / FRENCH ROMANTIC

The misty reed beds of the swampy lowlands of Avalon hold the mysteries of magic and power in shadow. Here, the once-goddess, once-fairy Morgan la Fey embraces the hidden things in darkness, nurturing their secret histories and desires, healing the wounds that are easily reopened and enacting power via the barely lit pathways that enable her to maneuver around the strictures of the expected. Here, where water meets Earth and both feed each other, the veil between the worlds—between tame and wild, between the known and the Other—grows thin. What we see here is only half seen, half trusted, and after we have followed Morgan herself down this wild path of knowing, we return healed but unable to tell if reality was reflected there or if it was simply imitated.

As above . . .

GODDESSES AND SYMBOLS

There is perhaps no figure depicted in *Pistis Sophia: The Goddess Tarot* that has been through so many changes over the centuries as Morgan la Fey. She has variously been a beneficent healer, a fairy, a goddess, a sorceress, a poisoner, an incestuous lover, a maiden giving herself secretly to a lover, an ugly hag, a queen, a necromancer, and a shape-shifter. Unlike many similar figures, a chronological development for these changes cannot be identified—in the same century she may have been most of these things, and even a single author might cast her in significantly different lights. It is clear that Morgan is as changeable as the moon, having many faces and—just as the moon reflects the light of the sun—her character reflecting the ideologies and social values of the times of her authors. In many ways, this reflection is one of fearfulness, just like the moon's light is seen as twisting the known into something Other at night, something that cannot be trusted, or is half formed and unclear. Morgan la Fey is an Otherly character "upon whom fear of the unknown or unpredictable is projected, making her a receptacle for mysterious and negative, if not evil, aspects of ourselves" (Hebert 2013, 2). Even her name suggests an origin in an otherworld—"Morgan the fairy," supernatural in origin, yet bound to the mortal world.

In the Tarot, The Moon is often a card of fluctuation, hidden power, secrecy, magic, mystery, feminine wisdom, inner fears, and madness. It gently illuminates the boundaries between the tame and the wild, between civilization and the wasteland, and then blurs those boundaries. In this card, we are pulled into an otherworld, shown the eddies and currents that flow beneath the surface—often seen as the subconscious mind or an individual's inner mythical/mystical landscape—and given a space in which the beneficent and the malefic and all things in between exist together. This is reflected in the many faces of Morgan la Fey shown in the card image—as dancing maiden, nurturing mother, wise crone, and starry warrior. The symbol of the triple moon seen in the card image—the full moon buttressed by a waxing and waning moon—has come to be associated in the neopagan and New Age movements with the concept of the divine feminine as maiden, mother, and crone. However, there are more than three phases to the moon; importantly, there is a phase where it is dark and hidden in the night sky. This is the face of the Other, the shape-shifter, the face that defies categorization based on female biology. Here, Morgan la Fey resides as the quintessential representation of the Other, uncontrolled feminine power, magic, shape-shifting, deceit, and mystery. Just like the Moon in the Tarot, in the Arthurian tales she is:

> relegated to the edge of the narrative structure [and] remains an uncontrollable, powerful female figure —both Mother and Lover—who actually holds the entire Arthurian tradition together.... She is what is not acknowledged, what cannot be acknowledged (Pérez 2014, 14).

It is in her ownership of the liminal and the Other in the Arthurian myths that she brings about the necessary challenges or changes that drive the narrative of the tales forward or offer rebirth for the main character, Arthur.

Many scholars have posited an influence from Welsh and Irish mythology for the formation of the character of Morgan, specifically from the Irish war goddess, the Morrigan—shown as the starry, spear-wielding goddess in the upper right of the card image. Parallels between Morgan and other Celtic mythological figures, such as Macha and Modron, have been made, with Loomis calling her "a female pantheon in miniature" (Loomis 1945, 183–203). However, a historical link between the Morrigan and Morgan la Fey has yet to be proven. In fact, the first mention of Morgan la Fey by name in extant texts is found in Geoffrey of Monmouth's *Vita Merlini*, written ca. 1150, in which she is the leader of nine sisters who govern an otherworldly land:

> In that place nine sisters give laws by means of genial rule / To those who come to them from our lands. / She who is eminent among them is more informed in the skill of healing; / She exceeds her sisters with superior form. / Her name is Morgen and she knows what of advantages / All the grasses bear so that she might cure sick bodies. / There is also a skill familiar to her by which she knows how / to change her shape / And how to cut through the sky, just as Daedalus with new feathers (trans. in Hebert 2013, 22).

This Morgan is an honored woman who teaches mathematics to her sisters. This view of Morgan as a woman of learning may have influenced Sir Thomas Malory when he wrote *Le Morte Darthur* in the fifteenth century: He introduced her by saying she "was put to school in a nunnery, and there she learned so much that she was a great clerk of necromancy" (trans. in Cooper 1998, 6). This learned woman, according to

Monmouth, received the wounded Arthur and his knights after the fateful battle of Camlan and agreed to take him into her care so she might heal him in time. It is as the healer of Arthur in her magical or Otherworldly realm that Morgan la Fey is perhaps most well known, and she consistently appears at the end of his story to take him into her care. In this way, she is the custodian of his future rebirth and of the fluctuations of life and death, of cycles and the flows of nature. The place in which Morgan receives Arthur's wounded body was called the "island of apples" or "the Fortunate Isle" by Geoffrey of Monmouth, but the link between her and Avalon, the mythical place now commonly associated with her, was first made by Chrétien de Troyes and Étienne de Rouen in the late twelfth century. Rouen's *Draco Normannicus* says the following:

> The wounded Arthur seeks plants there from his sister, / The holy island of Avalon holds them. / Here the eternal nymph Morgan receives her brother, / Cares for, nourishes [and] renews him, making him immortal (trans. in Hebert 2013, 30).

Rouen here granted to Morgan some divinity and magical power, calling her a nymph and suggesting that not only is she immortal, but that she has the power to give immortality to her wounded brother. Like many other writers, he also gave her great knowledge of medicine and healing. Only a few decades later, Gerald of Wales wrote in his *Speculum Ecclesiae* (ca. 1216) that Morgan was imagined as "some fantastic goddess" by the Britons, and that she took Arthur to Avalon to heal him so that he may return to rule the Britons again. He went into more detail in his *De Instructione Principis* (ca. 1223), where he explained that Avalon is now called Glastonbury, which is "entirely sown with swamps, like an island, for which reason it was called Inis Avallon by the Britons, that is, the apple-bearing island." He then called Morgan the "noble mother, ruler, and patron of those parts" (trans. in Hebert 2013, 35). Morgan's divine nature was also commented on in *Sir Gawain and the Green Knight*, the late-fourteenth-century Middle English chivalric romance, in which she is called "Morgan the Goddess" (trans. in Harrison 1998, 87).

Morgan's proficiency as a healer is a common thread through many of the earlier sources. In Chrétien de Troyes's *Erec et Enide* (ca. 1170), an ointment made by Morgan is described as so strong that:

> within a week it would completely cure and heal the wound being treated, whether in the ligaments or in the joints, provided the ointment was applied daily (trans. in Staines 1990, 53).

The same author called her "Morgan the Wise" and described an ointment that could heal the mind of any illness; thus, Morgan la Fey is given the power to heal both the body and the mind. This ability to heal disorders, illnesses, and wounds is interesting when considered alongside the relegation of Morgan la Fey to the Other and the unknown—The Moon of the Tarot is a place in which disorders, psychoses, past trauma and recurrent, cyclical issues are found, but it is also the place in which they can be healed or addressed. This card represents wounds that are easily reopened, past hurts that sometimes resurface, just as Arthur's wounds were sometimes said to break open afresh every year (Wade 2011, 49). Morgan tended to these wounds every time, just as The Moon offers us a space to address our issues safely, without judgment or limitation.

Despite her ability to tend to the sick and injured, Morgan became associated with places that are opposed to civilization and the chivalry of Arthur's court: in the *Vulgate* and *Post-Vulgate*, she became linked to the forests that exemplified wildness and ambiguity; this connection:

> adds another dimension of meaning: the forest becomes a place of ambiguity. It can be positive, negative, or neutral; a sanctuary, a nightmare, or a magical place (Hebert 2013, 40).

The Moon in the Tarot can likewise be positive, negative, or neutral—it can be a space for healing and finding wisdom, a landscape of nightmares, or a call to the Other. Although Morgan is undoubtedly a healer, some texts describe her as using her knowledge to also poison and cause harm. In the story of Alexander the Orphan, Morgan anoints Alexander's wounds with an unguent that makes them worse, and uses this to manipulate him into promising he will do anything she wants, repaying his promise by healing him and taking him to her castle to be her lover. She also drugs Lancelot's wine in order to give him nightmares about his lover, Guinevere, being unfaithful to him, and keeps him in her castle by blowing a powder into his nose that makes him too ill to leave (Larrington 2006, 18–19).

Morgan la Fey is a distinctly malefic force in many of the texts, including the influential *Morte Darthur*. Malory tells of Morgan's attempts on Arthur's life, caused by her hatred of him, and her attempts to disgrace Guinevere by exposing her illicit affair with Lancelot. In these episodes, Morgan's actions convey the deception and trickery so often represented by The Moon: She tricks Arthur by having a replica of his magical scabbard—which protects the bearer from blood loss—made and stealing the real scabbard for her lover; she causes them to fight, neither knowing each other's identities, believing that Accolon would kill Arthur (he is unsuccessful). Later, she tries to kill Arthur by sending him the gift of a cloak that will burn alive the person who wears it (a trick that is prevented by another magical woman from the Arthurian world, Ninianne, the Lady of the Lake). In an attempt to shame Guinevere, she creates a magical drinking horn that will reveal infidelity in a woman by causing her to spill whatever she tries to drink from it—this drinking horn, however, is rerouted to King Mark of Cornwall, where it finds its way to his court and reveals that all but four of the ladies of his court have been unfaithful. Morgan doesn't always resort to magical means to expose Guinevere and Lancelot, however. She shows Arthur paintings that Lancelot has created that symbolically portray the mutual love between himself and Guinevere. Unlike The Sun of the Tarot, which utilizes direct illumination and unfettered, harsh facts, The Moon prefers to use hints, allusions, illusion, and deception to reveal truths.

Morgan's use of magic is a vital aspect of her character, whether she is depicted as a goddess, eternal nymph, fairy, or human. Unlike her earliest mentions in the twelfth century, however, sources from the thirteenth century onward begin to depict this magic as malefic and evil and to associate it with Morgan's outward appearance and behavior. In the *Vulgate* and *Post-Vulgate*, she

> knew more about witchcraft and spells than any other woman; and because of her keen interest in such things, she gave up and forsook all dealings with people and lived day and night in far-off forests, so that many people never spoke of her as a woman but rather called her Morgan the Goddess (trans. in Rosenberg 1993, 305).

In the same cycle of texts she appears in one of Lancelot's dreams as the leader of a group of devils. In the *Suite de Merlin*, her association with magic and devils led to her becoming ugly:

> Morgan took the prize for beauty over all who were there that day. Unquestionably she was a beautiful girl up to the time she began to learn enchantments and magic charms; but once the enemy entered her and she was inspired with sensuality and the devil, she lost her beauty so completely that she became very ugly, nor did anyone think her beautiful after that, unless he was under a spell (quoted in Larrington 2006, 25–26).

This ugly appearance has been seen by several commentators as a link to the motif of the Loathly Lady that recurs throughout Arthurian stories. This dichotomy and interchangeability of ugly hag / beautiful maiden can be seen as reflective of The Moon, which can present a beneficent, beautiful face of nurture and healing yet can also bring with it associations of maleficence and ugliness: Consider the notion of lunacy, werewolves, and other creatures that come out only at night. That Morgan, and The Moon in the Tarot, can comfortably accommodate both these faces demonstrates the potential danger of uncontrolled female power in the medieval world.

Alongside her magical abilities, Morgan is specifically attributed with the ability to shapeshift, which reminds us of the fluctuating nature of The Moon. In *Le Morte Darthur*, Morgan transforms herself and her retinue into stone figures in order to escape Arthur; in the *Vita Merlini*, she is said to be able to change herself into a bird; in a twelfth-century poem by Hartmann von Aue, *Erec*, she can change a man into a bird or other animal, and can also walk on water, fly, control birds, beasts, and evil spirits, and enlist dragons, fish, and devils to aid her (Lupak 2007, 462).

Malory does not outline a reason for Morgan's hatred of Arthur, but other texts explain her hatred of Guinevere. In these, Morgan had an illicit relationship with Guinevere's cousin, Guiomar. Guinevere objected to the match, believing Morgan an unsuitable wife for her cousin, and convinced Guiomar to reject Morgan, who was heartbroken. This theme of illicit love recurs throughout Arthurian legends, reminding us that The Moon offers a light by which secrets can be made—in particular lover's trysts.

Although Morgan is frequently an outright enemy to the court of Arthur and all it represents, her actions being those of a villainous enemy, many scholars have pointed out that her acts of aggression can be seen as challenges for the knights that will allow them to grow in some way; they also question the role and function of chivalry and its boundaries and place challenges on the knights of Arthur's court when Arthur himself is too afraid to do so. Thus, Morgan acts as teacher and initiator (Hebert 2013). In the same way, The Moon, while presenting a landscape of fear and nightmares, may allow us to initiate ourselves into deeper mysteries by walking its wild, untamed path—if we can distinguish between truth and falsehood, light and shadow, imitation and reflection.

... *So below*

DIVINATORY MEANINGS

Falling between the other celestial bodies in the Tarot—Star and Sun—The Moon also deals with motifs of illumination and the nature of truth. Unlike the other two cards, however, in The Moon, truth is subjective and to be sought on the liminal edges between reality and fantasy. It calls the querent to take the shadowy, unknown paths instead of the paths most well trodden, and to listen to the dangerous, wild aspects of themselves and others. It represents secret knowledge, illicit wisdom and experiences, and trickery, in which learning is disguised in half truths and deceit. It initiates through deception and pulls forth the uncivilized, uncultivated aspects of the self, bringing them to the surface in all their ugly, strange glory.

In a reading, this card often indicates deception or secrecy; it may suggest an illicit relationship, being charged with a secret, or maintaining the mystery of the self or a project. It urges the querent to play their cards close to their chest for now, but also to look to others for hidden agendas and secret motives. It advises the querent to look beneath the obvious and try to identify the patterns and recurring themes of something—what keeps coming back to haunt them? Sometimes, it might also suggest a fluctuating situation, people and projects that keep changing. The querent is advised to take a flexible approach if they want to be able to keep track of things.

Spiritually, The Moon can point to initiation into the mysteries through immersion in the wild, in the Other, in the nightmare realm of our imaginations. Sometimes, it says, revelation is not about finding *the* truth but about peeling back the layers of fantasy to discover *a* truth. It can also be a card of magic, the divine feminine, and modern pagan religion—such as Wicca—in which the moon is an important symbol. Emotionally, this card indicates a deeply changeable heart, fickleness of feeling, and instability, perhaps mood swings. Thus, it might represent changes in the female body—such as puberty or menopause.

Negatively aspected, The Moon is completely untrustworthy and represents lies, malicious deceit, hidden pain, past trauma, or old wounds resurfacing.

KEYWORDS

Fluctuation, change, flux, unstable emotions, shifting personalities or nature; fantasy; the divine feminine; past trauma, old wounds resurfacing; the wild, nightmare, illusion, reflection; secrecy, lover's trysts, illicit affairs

XIX THE SUN

Amaterasu
JAPANESE SHINTO

Out of the Heavenly Rock-Cave, Amaterasu-ō-Mikami emerges. Rushing out to greet the celebrations and view her beautiful reflection in the mirror before her, her golden rays illuminate the long-darkened skies of Japan. Her kimono is the fiery colors of the life-giving sun—red, white, and gold—and the rising sun emblem adorns her back. In the background, the goddess Ame-no-Uzume dances in front of the company of deities, banging a drum and showing her genitalia to cause a stir and entice Amaterasu from her cave. The beautiful sun goddess's rays of light are reflected into the sky as she rises higher and higher, blessing the rice fields and the lands beneath her with life and sustenance. As she emerges, a great cry from the company of deities rings out: "Ahare! Ahare!" ("The sky is now illuminated!").

As above . . .

GODDESSES AND SYMBOLS

Amaterasu-ō-Mikami (also called Ōhiru-menomuchi-no-kami) is the Japanese Shinto deity of the sun. The religion of Shinto is the native religion of Japan and was the country's state religion until the First World War. Its nature has changed substantially since its origins and has been particularly affected by its contact with Buddhism from the sixth century CE onward, continuing to evolve since then. However, many of the deities (called *kami*, a word that is better translated as "spirit" or "essence") of ancient Shinto have remained popular and intrinsic in its modern form. Amaterasu is one such deity. Not only is she popular and important because of her nature as *kami* of the sun, but she is also the root of the imperial lineage and ancestry. In the *Kojiki* we are told that her great-great-great-grandson became the first emperor of Japan; her grandson descended to Earth to pacify and unite Japan (Chamberlain 1919, 129), and his great-grandson became Emperor Jim-mu (Chamberlain 1919, 159–88).

There are two main sources for the myths of Amaterasu—the *Kojiki* and the *Nihon Shoki*. The former forms what is perhaps the most comprehensive collection of what was previously a disparate set of folk myths and tales. The latter is more concerned with historical events and matters of imperial lineage than with the creation of the *kami*. A third source, the *Kogo Shūi*, completed around 806 CE, mentions Amaterasu more briefly and formally than the earlier two. In the *Kojiki*, Amaterasu was born from the left eye of the male creator, Izanagi, as he washed himself in a river

(Chamberlain 1919, 46), while in the *Nihon Shoki*, she was consciously created by Izanagi and his wife, Izanami (see Death), through sexual intercourse (Ashton 1896, Book 1). The *Kogo Shūi* follows the *Nihon Shoki* but emphasizes that Amaterasu's lineage leads directly to the imperial line of the emperor (Kato and Hoshino 1926, 24) and that the *kami* involved in enticing Amaterasu from her cave dwelling are ancestors of other lineages.

All the sources agree on the course of events of the particular myth illustrated in this card. In this story, Amaterasu's brother, Susano-o-no-Mikoto (also called His-Swift-Impetuous-Male-Augustness), the *kami* of storms, ravaged his sister's rice fields by breaking up the irrigation system and filling up the ditches, and smeared excrement on the walls of her dining hall. At first, Amaterasu forgave him this misbehavior, believing that Susano-o was simply expressing his dissatisfaction (Chamberlain 1919, 62). However, Susano-o continued his ravages, and, one night, while Amaterasu sat in her weaving hall with her handmaidens, he flayed a colt alive and threw it through the roof of Amaterasu's hall, whereupon it frightened the handmaidens so much that they fled or, in some versions, died of fear. (In the *Kojiki* version, the maidens' weaving implements pierced their genitalia, and they subsequently died.) Disgusted and angered by Susano-o's despicable actions, Amaterasu fled and concealed herself in the Heavenly Rock-Cave, sealing herself in:

> Whereupon Amaterasu-ō-Mikami was greatly incensed, and entering into the Heavenly Rock-Cave, closed its door and concealed herself therein. Consequently, the eternal night of darkness prevailed, so that no one could distinguish between the day and the night (Kato and Hoshino 1926, 19).

This darkness continued for several months. The land started to wither and die, along with men, women, and children, and the *kami* began to worry. They called together a council of *kami* to decide what to do, and after much discussion they formulated a plan to entice Amaterasu out of her cave and thus return the life-giving sun to the Earth. They transplanted a sacred sakaki tree with five hundred branches in front of the Heavenly Rock-Cave and hung upon it beautiful jewels and swords of the finest craftsmanship. Before the door of the cave they placed a mirror, and then the entire company of *kami* began to make noise: they made the sounds of celebration, joy, dancing, and worship. Ame-no-Uzume (also called Her-Augustness-Heavenly-Alarming-Female) danced wildly before the cave mouth, standing on an upturned bathtub (Kato and Hoshino 1926, 21) and lifting her skirts for all the *kami* to see, causing them to laugh raucously. Upon hearing this, Amaterasu peeked out of the cave and inquired as to why there was such celebration in the dark night of the world. The first thing she saw was the mirror and thus her own beautiful reflection, and she emerged from the cave, drawn ever closer by her own light. As she did so, light returned to the world and life with it. The company of *kami* rejoiced, crying out "Ahare! Ahare!" (A cry signifying that the sky is now illuminated), "Ana omoshiroshi!" ("O how delightful it is again clearly to see one another's faces!"), and "Ana tanoshi!" ("What joy to dance with outstretched hands!") (Kato and Hoshino 1926, 23).

It is worth noting that the items hung upon the sacred sakaki tree (jewels, swords, and the mirror) became the emblems of the imperial house of Japan. This, coupled with Amaterasu's great-great-great-grandson becoming the first emperor, means that every emperor of Japan was regarded as the descendent of Amaterasu, and his relationship with her was a special one. The imperial court was modeled on Amaterasu's court, and the emperor is thought to have reenacted the main myth of Amaterasu's emergence from the cave in a ritual called "calling back the lost soul of the Emperor" (Waida 1976, 337–41). (For more on the intimate and complex relationship between Amaterasu and the emperor, see Brown 2000, 101–17.)

It is possible that this myth intentionally coincides Amaterasu's hiding and emergence with certain festivals of the Japanese year. We are told that it is around the time of the year's first rice harvest festival that Susano-o smeared excrement on Amaterasu's feast hall and caused her to conceal herself in the Heavenly Rock-Cave (Chamberlain 1919, 61, n. 4). The *Yengishiki* (a collection of ancient Shinto rituals) gives its first ritual for Amaterasu to begin on the "17th day of the 6th moon of the year, as the morning sun goes up in glory." The final ritual ends "as the evening sun goes down on the last day of the watery moon of this year" (Horne 2006). These rituals aimed to cleanse those present of the sins that Susano-o committed against Amaterasu that caused her to take refuge in the Heavenly Rock-Cave. Thus we can speculate that appointing the rituals to this time of the year was to ensure that Amaterasu would emerge out of the cave at the end of the watery season.

The image of the sun emerging out of darkness is a powerful one. However, there is some speculation as to whether Amaterasu was originally a solar deity at all: as Lotte Motz pointed out, the goddess has not kept any of the usual qualities of a sun deity. She is not golden, does not ride across the sky, and is not greeted at sunrise, and her festivals follow the agricultural calendar instead of a solar one (Motz 1997, 176). Fortunately, we have not chosen Amaterasu for The Sun on the basis of her attributes as a solar deity, but instead because her emergence from the cave amid celebration, returning light to the world, is fitting for this card. This is a card of renewed illumination, the light of truth allowing us to see clearly what is before us. The light of Amaterasu dispels confusion and ignorance, lies and deceit, and allows humankind to soar to new heights of spiritual and intellectual understanding.

. . . *So below*

DIVINATORY MEANINGS

The Sun is often a welcome card in any reading, bringing with it the blessings of illumination, celebration, joy, and warmth. It is a particularly positive card in relation to the communities we build for ourselves, as it points to celebrations with others and sharing our joy in the world. The illuminating power of The Sun in the Tarot is infectious, spreading uncontrolled and quickly, dispelling all darkness.

As such, in a reading where the querent is experiencing uncertainty or feels like something is being hidden from them, The Sun brings a promise that all will be made clear and that a path will soon be placed before the querent. Where there were once lies, now there is only truth. Where there was once a lack of clarity, now there is certainty.

The Sun also brings into a reading the possibility of a spiritual awakening or improvement. Just as we look to light to guide our way, so The Sun offers a divine illumination of the spirit, mind, heart, and soul. It reminds the querent that they are constantly evolving, and that opportunities for their spiritual growth abound at this time. In the everyday world, evolution is still indicated by this card: the querent can expect to soon soar to great heights of achievement and the joy that it brings.

Just as the sun gives the warmth and light required for all life on our planet to grow, so The Sun in the Tarot shines a life-giving light on any reading in which it appears. Where this card is found, other cards can be expected to take root and grow, the promise of their fulfilment being accelerated or made more certain. Everywhere The Sun touches in the querent's life can be expected to see an unparalleled period of growth; inspiration and a rush of renewed energy from the querent will help move things closer to completion.

This card brings a great deal of happiness and positivity to a reading. It speaks of optimism and reasons for the querent to be joyful. Where things are looking difficult or gloomy, the querent is asked to consider what aspects of their life give them joy, and move toward them. It is time for the querent to leave behind the cave of shadows and walk toward the path of light.

Negatively aspected, however, The Sun illuminates everything, even that which the querent does not want to be illuminated. It represents something coming to light regardless of the pain it might cause, and puts everything in the harsh light of day.

KEYWORDS

Illumination and enlightenment; spiritual growth; forward movement and progress; unparalleled periods of growth; immense joy and happiness; clarity and clarification; moving away from uncertainty; illumination of truth; achievement; community celebrations

XX REBIRTH
(JUDGMENT)

Inanna
SUMERIAN

Deep within the Earth, in the realm of Ereškigal the goddess of death, Inanna's body lies broken, battered, and bruised. She has been stripped completely of her power, her finery, and her queenly status on her descent into the underworld and executed by Ereškigal, her body hung on a meat hook to rot. But from this painful journey, with its trials and sufferings, from the depths of darkness, Inanna is reborn to the world above, renewed and replenished, her power and status returned to her as she rises upward. Nothing can stop her bright light from reaching all the way to the Heaven Above as she rises, like a phoenix from the ashes, from the Heaven Below, removing herself from the shackles of her broken body and entrapment in darkness.

As above . . .

GODDESSES AND SYMBOLS

The Sumerian goddess Inanna was called by many names and epithets: "Great Lady of Heaven," "Holy Priestess of Heaven," "First Daughter of the Moon," "Loud Thundering Storm," "Lady of the Evening," "Honored Counselor," "Ornament of Heaven," "The Brave One," and "Amazement of the Lands." In her myths, she is a powerful warrior, a holy priestess, a great queen, a mother, a lover, a sister, a daughter, and the bringer of all the sacred laws and wisdom to the city of Uruk. One of the myths tells of how she visits Enki, the god of wisdom, at his temple in Eridu and gets him drunk. Whilst drunk, he gifts her with the sacred *me*, the attributes of civilization, and she returns to her home city as a hero and queen (Wolkstein and Kramer 1983, 146–50).

Her passionate, fierce, and powerful personality in the Sumerian pantheon make it all the more surprising when she descends to the underworld and is killed by Ereškigal, being left to rot on a meat hook in the dark until Ninshubar alerts Enki to her loss and Inanna is rescued. The myth states that

> From the great above she set her mind toward the great below,
>
> The goddess, from the great above, she set her mind toward the great below,
>
> Inanna, from the great above, she set her mind toward the great below.

> My Lady abandoned heaven, abandoned Earth, to the netherworld she descended
> ... (Pritchard 1969, 53).

For such a goddess to fall from such a height to the great below is a long fall indeed, and this is perhaps why the story of Inanna's descent into the underworld is one of the most important texts in the corpus of Sumerian religious literature. The text itself is reconstructed from thirteen tablets and several fragments, which were inscribed in the first half of the second millennium BCE. The reason for Inanna's descent to the netherworld is widely believed to be to locate and revive her dead lover, Dumuzi, yet the text itself is unclear on her reasons.

When she arrived at the gates of the netherworld, Inanna told the gatekeeper that she had come to witness the funeral rites for Ereškigal's husband, the recently deceased Gulugunna, though no other mention of his death or funeral is made. Before she set her feet on the path to the netherworld, Inanna arrayed herself with the seven *me* (Kramer translates this as "ordinances") that she gained from Enki, which seem to be contained within physical objects that represent various aspects of her power, royalty, holiness, and desirability. Upon her head she placed the *shugurra*, the crown of the steppe; around her neck she placed small lapis beads; upon her breast she arrayed a double strand of beads; upon her chest she wore a breastplate; on her wrist she placed a ring of gold; in her hand she carried a lapis measuring rod and line; she clothed her body in the royal robes. Thus, in full possession of all her power and status, Inanna arrived at the lapis gates of the netherworld, where she was greeted by the gatekeeper, Neti, who asked

> If thou art Inanna of the place where the sun rises,
>
> Why, pray, hast thou come to the land of no return?
>
> On the road whose traveller returns not, how hath thy heart led thee? (Pritchard 1969, 54)

This question immediately informs us that nobody truly returns from the road of rebirth, for the self that "returns" is not the self that first set foot on the journey.

When Neti informed his mistress, Ereškigal—whom Inanna called her elder sister—that Inanna had arrayed herself in the seven *me* and arrived at their door, Ereškigal instructed Neti to allow her to pass through the seven gates of the netherworld, but at each gate she was to remove one of the seven *me* from her person. Thus, the seven items that represented Inanna's status, power, and holiness—the very items that signified her selfhood—were stripped from her completely. These aspects of the ego must be removed before the transformation processes of rebirth can begin to take place. If they are not removed when necessary, the beautiful robes, the crown, the breastplate, and the jewels will become chains holding us back, binding us to stagnation, blocking our transition. Thus, Inanna entered the throne room of Ereškigal naked, bowed low, and ready for rebirth. She entered the womb of the netherworld as naked as the day she exited from her mother's womb. Meador comments that the descent myth . . . strip[s] the goddess/woman of all her possessions, all her power, everything which registered in her psyche as a familiar article belonging to her former life. Her dependable habits, her daily chores, her manner of dressing, the objects she cherished, all are gone. She is stripped down to zero (Meador 1992, 43).

As soon as she entered, the Anunnaki (the seven judges) pronounced judgment upon her, and upon their word Inanna was killed and her body hung upon a stake to rot. The old self, the body that contained the spirit and shackled it, has been destroyed in the phoenix flames. It is interesting that the original name for this Major Arcana is "Judgment," which still plays a role in the nature of this card—which we have renamed "Rebirth." Without judgment and the ability to discriminate, we are unable to let go of the aspects of the self that hold us back. The judgment of the Anunnaki in the myth, therefore, and the accusatory nature of Inanna's destruction at the hands of Ereškigal, remind us that we must often pronounce harsh judgment upon parts of our selves and egos, any unwanted and habitual thought patterns and behaviors.

For three days and three nights the corpse of Inanna hung, rotting, on the stake. When her messenger, Ninshubar, realized that Inanna had been lost, he went to the other gods and asked for help in retrieving her. First he went to Enlil and Nanna, who both refused to help:

My daughter has asked for the great above, has asked for the great below,

Inanna has asked for the great above, has asked for the great below,

The ordinances of the netherworld, the . . . ordinances,

The ordinances—she has reached their place (Pritchard 1969, 56).

These gods seem to refuse to help because Inanna has chosen this path herself, has asked for the netherworld and received it; they also suggest that the seven *me* that she received from Enki came originally from the netherworld and that she has returned them to their place. So Ninshubar went to Enki to ask for help, and he—distraught at what they fear has happened—created two genderless beings (called *kurgurru* and *kalaturru*) from the dirt beneath his fingernails. He instructed them to sneak into the netherworld "like flies," where they would find Ereškigal crying in the pain of labor, her hair unkempt, and no sheet covering her. There, they should mimic her cries. When they did so, perceiving this mimicry as sympathy, Ereškigal would offer them a gift. They were to refuse all offers and to ask instead for the corpse of Inanna. To ensure that Inanna rose from death, Enki supplied the *kurgurru* and *kalaturru* with the food and water of life.

The genderless beings entered the netherworld, where they did as they were bid. They found Ereškigal moaning like a woman in labor, which has been interpreted by some as the birth pains experienced by Ereškigal that are necessary to bring about the rebirth of Inanna. As the one who pronounced death upon Inanna, and the one who kept her rotting beneath the Earth, Ereškigal had instigated the transformation process of rebirth, as well as the necessary gestation period. The genderless beings were gifted with Inanna's rotting corpse, upon which they sprinkled the water of life and into which they placed the food of life. The text simply reads, "Inanna arose. Inanna ascends from the nether world, the Anunnaki fled" (Pritchard 1969, 56). Not only did Inanna arise from the underworld, reborn and renewed, but she also expelled the forces of judgment.

Modern interpretations of the myth of Inanna's descent to the netherworld focus on the fact that her death at the hands of Ereškigal and her prior stripping and humiliation are comparable to the downward spirals many of us experience at our darkest times. Thus, the myth of Inanna and her subsequent rebirth from such a place tells us that these experiences can be cauldrons of rebirth, phoenix flames in which we are to burn so that we may bring about our own rebirth. The force that destroys us (Ereškigal) also brings about our birth and transition, and, whether it is voluntarily or forcefully, we are made to break free from the shackles and chains that hold us back from change.

. . . So below

DIVINATORY MEANINGS

When Rebirth appears in a reading, the querent should expect a complete transformation, a process of rebirth, and the breaking free from anything that previously held them back. With this card come the flames that burn away the old self, allowing the new self and the spirit to rise free into opportunity and limitless awareness, like a phoenix from the flames. It also brings with it the message that just as it is Inanna's sister, her own flesh and blood, that brings her rebirth to fruition through her own labor pains, so we hold within ourselves the seeds and keys to our rebirth. First, however, we must step into the destructive flames—sometimes this happens willingly, and sometimes it is forced upon us. Other cards in the reading and the context of the question may indicate whether this path is one the querent walks voluntarily or without choice.

Rebirth advises the querent to let go of habitual modes of thought and habits and to view what comes to them as an opportunity for freedom. With Rebirth comes a complete breath of fresh air, an opportunity to slough the old, worn-out skin that bears upon it so many scars and rough edges, and a path ahead that is waiting for feet to tread upon it for the first time.

This card can often indicate a spiritual awakening or religious rebirth, rather than just a mundane one, and it also suggests that the querent is striving toward a higher awareness or goal. In a reading about projects, career, or work, Rebirth can point to the freedom to try something new, or an opportunity that will challenge the querent but help them grow.

Negatively aspected, Rebirth becomes a trial by fire. The querent may find themselves in a situation of being harshly judged by others or circumstances and held unfairly accountable, punished or treated accordingly.

KEYWORDS

Rebirth; reawakening; rejuvenation; transformation; awareness; aspirations, goals; liberation, freedom

XXI THE UNIVERSE

Nut
EGYPTIAN

In the heavens, made from stars and surrounded by the twelve signs of the zodiac in their order, the Egyptian sky goddess Nut performs a dual function: With her arms outstretched, she sees the sacred barge of Ra across the sky in its daily journey from dawn to dawn, traveling through the underworld and being born from the horizon once more; with her body, she receives the soul of the dead pharaoh, bringing him back to eternal life in the afterlife. The zodiac evokes a sense of time and its cyclical rather than linear nature, and the four sacred animals of the elements represent the manifestation of the physical world.

As above . . .

GODDESSES AND SYMBOLS

Nut is the Egyptian sky goddess who was said to bring forth the five gods and goddesses of creation—Isis, Osiris, Set, Nephthys, and Horus the Elder—as well as a number of other deities. She is described variously as the sister-wife of Seb, Geb, or Nu; these siblings were born from the sibling-lovers Shu and Tefnut ("air" and "moisture"), who were in turn born from the semen or saliva of the creator god Ra (Kaster 1995, 54). Many commentators view her simply as a personification of the night sky or the heavens, but as Susan Hollis shows, Nut plays an integral role in the creation of the universe, its continuation, and its renewal—she was the mother of the stars and the sun, both initially and with each new day (Hollis 1987, 496–503).

Commonly, images of Nut depict her as covered or surrounded by stars, sometimes colored blue or black to mimic the night sky, with her long body arched forward over the whole of creation. Her arms and legs are the four pillars of the Earth at the cardinal points. Often, a scene is played out within her arch (usually a scene related to the life of the deceased buried in the tomb, or a scene from the accompanying funerary texts), or her husband Geb is depicted lying beneath her—sometimes resting on his elbow and sometimes with an erect phallus pointing toward her. Images of Nut from the New Kingdom period in tombs and coffins also show the sun being swallowed by her in the evening in the west and being born from her in the morning in the east.

The cyclical journey of the sun god Ra on his sacred barge, Sektet, across the daytime sky and into the underworld at night is a theme repeatedly written about in the *Pyramid Texts* and the *Book of the Dead*. Ra was believed to have four aspects relating to the four stages of the day: Kephri at dawn, Ra at midday, Atum at dusk, and Sokar at midnight (these names differ in some texts, and not all the stages are mentioned in some hymns, such as the "Hymn to Ra at Rising," from the *Papyrus of Qenna* (Budge 1989, 4–7). The journey into the night half of the day is often divided into twelve "hours," during which Ra enters the Duat (underworld) and faces different obstacles and challenges:

> When all the land is black, the sun bark of Ra passes through the twelve hour-divisions of night in Duat. At eventide, when the god is Tum, he is old and very frail. Five-and-seventy invocations are chanted to give him power to overcome the demons of darkness who are his enemies. He then enters the western gate, through which dead men's souls pass to be judged before Osiris (MacKenzie 1907, 11–12).

It is Nut that swallows Ra and Sektet at dusk, and his journey in the underworld takes place within her starry body (itself a representation of night), from which he is born as her son once more. As such, Nut is a goddess who brings about rebirth, cycles, and eternal life. Every ending (dusk) leads to a new beginning (dawn), and this cycle is never ending as long as there is a universe:

> The sun god is reborn in the twelfth hour-division. He enters the tail of the mighty serpent, which is named "Divine Life," and issues from its mouth in the form of Khepera, which is a beetle. Those who are with the god are reborn also. . . . He is then received by Nut, goddess of the heavens; he is born of Nut and grows in majesty, ascending to high noon (MacKenzie 1907, 14).

Throughout the history of ancient Egypt, the royal house of the pharaoh was bound to the gods Ra and Osiris—Ra as the continually reborn and eternal Sun, and Osiris as ruler of Egypt and later ruler of the underworld (at which point the pharaoh was also considered to be his son, Horus, new ruler of Egypt). As such, it is not surprising to find the pharaoh—in particular the deceased pharaoh—identified with, and as, Ra himself, being swallowed by Nut in the west in the evening (at death) and being reborn from her as her eternal child in the east (the afterlife). This identification is clear in the *Pyramid Texts*, where the pharaoh is commanded to

> sit on this throne of Re that [he] may give orders to the gods, because [he is] Re who came forth from Nut who bears Re daily, and [the king is] born daily like Re (Utterance 606:1688. All *Pyramid Texts* references are to the Faulkner 1969 translation.).

In this text, Nut plays an integral role in the establishment of the deceased pharaoh's soul in the afterlife:

> O Great One who came into being in the sky, you have achieved power, you have achieved strength, and have filled every place with your beauty; the entire land is yours. Take possession of it, for you have enclosed the Earth and

all things within your embrace, and you have set this King as an Imperishable Star who is in you (Utterance 432:782).

Here the pharaoh becomes a star in the company of stars of Nut's body, eternal and above the Earth. This particular passage ends with the pharaoh thus "given all life, stability, prosperity, health, joy like Re, [he] lives forever." Upon his death, he is depicted as being met with joy and love by Nut, who says that she has already borne him once:

Behold, she comes to meet you, does the Beautiful West, meet you with her lovely tresses, and she says, "Here comes he whom I have borne, whose horn is upstanding, the eye-painted Pillar, the Bull of the sky!" (Utterance 254:282–83.

The title "Bull of Heaven" is often used to describe Nut's husband, and the word "bull" is also used to indicate brother or son. Here, the pharaoh is Nut's lover, brother, and son, returning to the cosmic womb whence he originally came.

Further, the deceased pharaoh variously accompanies Ra in his barge through the Duat—"[He] sits with those who row Re" (Utterance 252:274) or undergoes the journey through the twelve hours of the Duat himself, as Ra:

[He] is conducted on the roads of Kophrer, [he] rests in life in the West, and the dwellers in the Netherworld [Duat] attend him. The King shines anew in the East (Utterance 257:306).

I appear as Nefertem, as the lotus-bloom which is at the nose of Re; he will issue from the horizon daily the gods will be cleansed at the sight of him (Utterance 249:266).

At times it is unclear whether the text is speaking about Ra or the pharaoh, suggesting that the differentiation between the two is unimportant to the purpose of the text; later, the name of the pharaoh is put in the place of Ra and Osiris in their functions and relationships to the other gods. The pharaoh has become divine after death (Utterances 1–11).

Although it was originally the pharaoh whom Nut embraced after death, later coffins and tombs show that anybody of any rank who could afford such a burial was also embraced by her. The coffin of an Egyptian woman named Cleopatra from the second century CE in the Salt Collection of the British Museum bears an interior lid (which would be stretching over the deceased, just as Nut stretched over creation) upon which Nut is dressed in contemporaneous costume, her hands at the head of the coffin and her feet at the base, with the signs of the zodiac arrayed in order around the edges.

The inner coffin of the priest Hornedjitef from the same collection, dated to the third century BCE, bears the figure of Nut on the interior lid (once again, facing the deceased). Upon her body is inscribed chapter 89 of the *Book of the Dead* ("The Chapter of Causing the Soul to Be United to Its Body in the Underworld"), which bears a vignette of the deceased as a mummy lying on a bier, his soul in the form of a human-headed bird flying above him, bearing a *shen*—the symbol of eternity—in its claws (Budge 1989, 279). This has been reproduced at the base of the Universe card in a form that suggests the deceased is also being born from the body of Nut. To the left of Nut on Hornedjitef's coffin lid is a list of planets and decans, and to her right are the constellations of the Northern Hemisphere. The lid of the coffin of Soter, from Thebes in the second century CE, shows Nut with the morning and evening suns in barges flanking her head, and at her sides are the signs of the zodiac.

We have taken inspiration from these and other coffins for The Universe. The zodiac around Nut suggests the progression of time and the cyclical nature of life and death: the zodiac begins in Aries and ends in Pisces but goes back again to Aries; the decans of the zodiac last for ten days each but begin again when the entire year rolls around (there are thirty-six decans, equaling the 360 degrees of the entire solar year). In our image, the barge of Ra does not flank Nut's head but instead is held aloft by her in its four stages, and the four elemental animals at each corner represent the elements just before they reach synthesis, as well as the elements in manifestation: both this card and Nut are beginnings and endings, and the liminal point at which destruction becomes manifestation and vice versa.

. . . *So below*

DIVINATORY MEANINGS

In a reading, The Universe can suggest a wide variety of possible meanings. It is vital to consider this card in the context of the question and surrounding cards.

Most often, it indicates the cyclical nature of an ending or beginning, suggesting that although the querent may be reaching the conclusion of something, they should be aware that the seeds of what is yet to come will already be planted within that conclusion. It could be that something needs to be concluded in order for it to become the driving force of a new project or goal, or perhaps the results of one thing will naturally lead onto the initiation of another thing. Manifestation will be born from completion.

As the last card in the Major Arcana, The Universe also indicates accomplishment and achievement. If the reading is about whether something will be successful or fruitful, this card is most welcome, indicating a positive attainment of a goal or victory of some kind. As it is found in the Major Arcana, the thing that has been completed successfully is also likely to be something significant for the querent. As such, The Universe can often signify the completion or attainment of an important life goal.

Often, The Universe brings to a reading issues of time and asks the querent how much time they are willing to give to something in order to see it through to completion. If accompanied by slow cards, completion could be a long way off. If accompanied by swift cards, however, such as The Chariot, completion and success are imminent.

Regardless of how long it takes, The Universe draws a line under something in a reading. It lays out the pattern of endings and beginnings and states very firmly that something will end and that something else will take its place. Like The Wheel, though, it also reminds the querent of the cyclical nature of life.

Sometimes this card can appear to signify synthesis of some kind; the querent may be advised to draw on several sources or resources to create something new from their synthesis. It can also represent the notion of everything finally coming together and making sense.

Negatively aspected, the Universe can represent an inability to move forward or accept an ending. It may also suggest that the querent is divided in several ways, unable to pull themselves together or bring everything they need together to form a conclusion.

KEYWORDS

The cyclical nature of time, endings and beginnings, completion of a cycle; synthesis; attainment and accomplishment; life goals being achieved, time

BIBLIOGRAPHY

Abiodun, Rowland. "Woman in Yoruba Religious Images." *African Languages and Cultures* 2, no. 1 (1989): 1–18.

Aeschylus. *Eumenides*. Translated by Alan H. Summerstein. Cambridge, UK: Cambridge University Press, 1989.

Alföldi, Andrew. "A Festival of Isis in Rome under the Christian Emperors of the Fourth Century." *Journal of Roman Studies* 28, no. 1 (1938): 88–90.

Anders, Ferdinand. *Codex Magliabecchiano CL XIII.3 (B.R. 232) Anon, vida de los Yndios*. Biblioteca Nazionale Centrale de Firenze (ca. 1560). Facsimile edition with commentary (Codices Selecti 23), 1970.

Anderson, Mary Margaret. "Thy Word in Me: On the Prayer of Union in St. Teresa of Avila's 'Interior Castle.'" *Harvard Theological Review* 99, no. 3 (2006): 329–54.

Anderson, Sherry Ruth, and Patricia Hopkins. *The Feminine Face of God: The Unfolding of the Sacred in Women*. New York: Bantam Books, 1992.

ap Iorwerth, Geraint. *Honest to Goddess: Russia, Sophia and the Celtic Soul*. Hampshire, UK: Crescent Books, 1998.

Apollodorus. *The Library of Greek Mythology*. Translated by Robin Hard. Oxford: Oxford University Press, 1997.

Apuleius. *The Golden Ass*. Translated by E. J. Kenney. London: Penguin Books, 2004.

———. *The Most Pleasant and Delectable Tale of the Marriage of Cupid and Psyche*. Translated by William Adlington. London: Chatto and Windus, 1914.

Ashton, W. G. *Nihongi: Chronicles of Japan from the Earliest Times to A.D. 697* (excerpts). London: Kegan Paul, 1896. Available online at www.sacred-texts.com/shi/index.htm.

———. *Shinto: The Ancient Religion of Japan*. Whitefish, MT: Kessinger, 2006.

Assman, Jan. *Religion and Cultural Memory: Ten Studies*. Translated by Rodney Livingstone. Stanford, CA: Stanford University Press, 2006.

Báez-Jorge, Félix. *Los oficios de las diosas* [The stations of the goddesses]. Xalapa, Mexico: Universidad Veracruzana, 1988.

Barguet, Paul. *Le livre des morts des anciens Égyptiens*. Paris: Cerf, 1967.

———. *Textes des sarcophages égyptiens*. Paris: Cerf, 1986.

Barr, Beth Allison. *The Pastoral Care of Women in Late Medieval England*. Suffolk, UK: Boydell, 2008.

Baudrillart, André. *Les divinités de la victoire en Grèce et en Italie*. Paris: Thorin, 1894.

Bentley, Toni. *Sisters of Salome*. New Haven & London: Yale University Press, 2002.

Benard, Elisabeth, and Beverly Moon, eds. *Goddesses Who Rule*. New York: Oxford University Press, 2000.

Berndt, C. H., and R. M. Berndt. *Sexual Behaviour in Western Arnhem Land*. Viking Fund Publications in Anthropology 16. New York: Wenner-Gren Foundation for Anthropological Research, 1951.

Betz, Hans Dieter, ed. *The Greek Magical Papyri in Translation, Including the Demotic Spells*. Chicago: University of Chicago Press, 1996.

Beyer, Stephen. *The Cult of Tara*. Stanford, CA: Stanford University Press, 1970.

Billington, Sandra, and Miranda Green, eds. *The Concept of the Goddess*. New York: Routledge, 1999.

Black, Jeremy, Anthony Green, and Tessa Rickards. *Gods, Demons, and Symbols of Ancient Mesopotamia*. Austin: University of Texas Press, 1992.

Blofield, John. *Bodhisattva of Compassion: The Mystical Tradition of Kwan Yin.* Boston: Shambhala, 1988.

Brinton, Daniel G., trans. *Rig Veda Americanus: Sacred Songs of the Ancient Mexicans, with a Gloss in Nahuatl.* Philadelphia: D. G. Brinton, 1890. Available online at www.sacred-texts.com/nam/aztec/rva/index.htm.

Brown, C. Mackenzie, trans. *The Song of the Goddess: The Devi Gita; Spiritual Counsel of the Great Goddess.* Albany: State University of New York Press, 2002.

———. "The Tantric and Vedāntic Identity of the Great Goddess in the Devī Gītā of the Devī-Bhāgavata Purāna." In *Seeking Mahādevī: Constructing the Identities of the Hindu Great Goddess.* Edited by Tracy Pintchman, 19–36. Albany: State University of New York Press, 2001.

Brown, Delmer M. "Sovereignty and the Great Goddess of Japan." In *Goddesses Who Rule.* Edited by Elisabeth Benard and Beverly Moon, 101–17. New York: Oxford University Press, 2000.

Brown, Karen McCarthy. *Mama Lola: A Vodou Priestess in Brooklyn.* Berkeley: University of California Press, 1991.

Buckley, Thomas, and Alma Gottlieb. *Blood Magic: The Anthropology of Menstruation.* Berkeley: University of California Press, 1988.

Budge, E. A. Wallis, trans. *The Book of the Dead.* London: Arkana, 1989.

———, trans. *The Book of the Dead: The Papyrus of Ani.* London: British Museum, 1895.

———, trans. *The Egyptian Heaven and Hell: Three Volumes Bound as One.* New York: Dover, 1996.

———. *Egyptian Magic.* London: Arkana, 1988.

———. *The Gods of the Egyptians.* Vol. 1. New York: Dover, 1969a.

———. *The Gods of the Egyptians.* Vol. 2. New York: Dover, 1969b.

———. *Legends of the Egyptian Gods.* New York: Dover, 1994.

Bulgakov, Sergei. *Sophia, the Wisdom of God: An Outline of Sophiology.* Hudson, NY: Lindisfarne, 1993.

Burkert, Walter. *Greek Religion.* Translated by John Raffar. Cambridge, MA: Harvard University Press, 1985.

Butterworth, G. W., trans. *Clement of Alexandria.* Loeb Classical Library 92. Cambridge, MA: Harvard University Press, 1919.

Campbell, David A., ed. and trans. *Greek Lyric, Volume IV: Bacchylides, Corinna, and Others.* Loeb Classical Library. Cambridge, MA: Harvard University Press, 1992.

———, ed. and trans. *Greek Lyric, Volume V: The New School of Poetry and Anonymous Songs and Hymns.* Loeb Classical Library. Cambridge, MA: Harvard University Press, 1994.

Campbell, Joseph. "The Four Functions of Myth." In *Inward Journey: The Thresholds of Mythology.* Audiobook. St. Paul. MN: HighBridge, 1996.

———. *The Hero with a Thousand Faces.* Princeton, NJ: Princeton University Press, 1949.

———. *The Masks of God.* Vol. 4, *Creative Mythology.* London: Souvenir, 2011.

———. *The Power of Myth.* New York: Anchor Books Doubleday, 1988.

Carmichael, Alexander. *Carmina Gadelica: Hymns and Incantations.* 6 vols. New York: Lindisfarne, 1994.

———. *Carmina Gadelica: Hymns and Incantations.* Vol. III. London: Oliver & Boyd, 1940.

———. *Carmina Gadelica: Hymns and Incantations.* Vol. IV. Edinburgh: Scottish Academic Press, 1970.

Carrasco, David. "Uttered from the Heart: Guilty Rhetoric among the Aztecs." *History of Religions* 39, no. 1 (1999): 1–31.

Carter, Angela. "Femmes Fatale" in *Shaking a Leg: Collected Writings* (ed.) Jenny Uglow. New York and London: Penguin, 1997.

Carty, Marcel. *The Vodou Religion*. Pittsburgh, PA: Dorrance, 2003.

Cashford, Jules, trans. *The Homeric Hymns*. London: Penguin Books, 2003.

Chadwick, Nora. *The Celts*. London: Penguin Books, 1974.

Chamberlain, Basil Hall, trans. *The Kojiki*. Tokyo: Kairyudo, 1919. Available online at www.sacred-texts.com/shi/kj/index.htm.

———, trans. *Ko-Ji-Ki or "Records of Ancient Matters."* Kobe, Japan: J. L. Thompson, 1932.

Chandola, Sudha. *Entranced by the Goddess: Folklore in North Indian Religion*. Loughborough, UK: Heart of Albion, 2007.

Chatwin, Bruce. *The Songlines*. London: Vintage Random House, 1998.

Chilton, Bruce, Darrell Bock, and Daniel M. Gurtner. *A Comparative Handbook to the Gospel of Mark*. Leiden, The Netherlands: Brill Academic, 2009.

Clark, Charlotte R. "The Egyptian Mother Goddess." *Metropolitan Museum of Art Bulletin*, n.s. 4, no. 9 (1946): 240–42.

Condren, Mary. *The Serpent and the Goddess: Women, Religion, and Power in Celtic Ireland*. New York: HarperCollins, 1989.

Conway, Geoffrey S., trans. *The Odes of Pindar*. London: J. M. Dent, 1972.

Cooper, Helen. *Le Morte Darthur: The Winchester Manuscript*. New York: Oxford University Press, 1998.

Cowan, James. *Aborigine Dreaming*. London: Thorsons, 2002.

———. *Myths of the Dreaming: Interpreting Aboriginal Legends*. Bridport, UK: Prism, 1994.

Cruden, Loren. *Coyote's Council Fire: Contemporary Shamans on Race, Gender, and Community*. Rochester, VT: Destiny Books, 1995.

Cusack, Carole. "Brigit: Goddess, Saint, 'Holy Woman,' and Bone of Contention." In *On a Panegyrical Note: Studies in Honour of Garry W Trompf*. Sydney, Australia: Department of Studies in Religion, University of Sydney, 2007.

Daniélou, Alain. *Gods of Love and Ecstasy: The Traditions of Shiva and Dionysus*. Rochester, VT: Inner Traditions, 1992.

Deren, Maya. *Divine Horsemen: The Living Gods of Haiti*. New York: McPherson, 2004.

Dio, Cassius. *Dio's Roman History VIII*. Translated by Earnest Cary. Cambridge, MA: Harvard University Press, 2001.

———. *Roman History*. 9 vols. Translated by Earnest Cary. Loeb Classical Library. Cambridge, MA: Harvard University Press, 1914–1927.

Durand-Forest, J. de, and Michel Graulich. "On Paradise Lost in Central Mexico." *Current Anthropology* 25, no. 1 (1984): 134–35.

Edkins, Rev. Joseph. *Chinese Buddhism: A Volume of Sketches, Historical, Descriptive, and Critical*. London: Kegan Paul, Trench and Trubner, 1893.

Edwards, Lee R. "The Labours of Psyche: Toward a Theory of Female Heroism." *Critical Enquiry* 6, no. 1 (1979): 33–49.

Ehrman, Bart D. *Truth and Fiction in the Da Vinci Code*. New York: Oxford University Press, 2004.

Electronic Text Corpus of Sumerian Literature (ETCSL). *A Hymn to Nanshe: Translation*. 2009. Available online at http://etcsl.orinst.ox.ac.uk/section4/tr4141.htm.

Erhardt, Michelle A., and Amy M. Morris, eds. *Mary Magdalene, Iconographic Studies from the Middle Ages to the Baroque*. Boston: Brill, 2012.

Eton Simpson, George. "The Belief System of Haitian Vodou." *American Anthropologist*, n.s. 47, no. 1 (1945): 35–59.

Evelyn-White, H. G., trans. *Hesiod, Homeric Hymns, Epic Cycle, Homerica*. Loeb Classical Library 57. London: William Heinemann, 1914.

Faulkner, R. O., trans. *The Ancient Egyptian Pyramid Texts*. Wiltshire, UK: Aris and Phillips, 1969.

Filan, Kenaz. *The Haitian Vodou Handbook: Protocols for Riding with the Lwa*. Rochester, VT: Destiny Books, 2007.

Fitch, Florence M. *Shinto: The Japanese Way of Worship*. Whitefish, MT: Kessinger, 2005.

Frankel, Valerie Estelle. *From Girl to Goddess: The Heroine's Journey through Myth and Legend*. Jefferson, NC: McFarland, 2010.

Frazer, James G., trans. *Apollodorus: The Library*. Loeb Classical Library 121 & 122. London: William Heinemann, 1921.

———, trans. *Pausanias's Description of Greece*. Vol. 5, *Commentary on Books IX, X, Addenda*. Whitefish, MT: Kessinger, 2010.

Fredrick, Serena. "The Sky of Knowledge: A Study of the Ethnoastronomy of the Aboriginal People of Australia." MA thesis, Department of Archaeology and Ancient History, University of Leicester, 2008.

Gleason, Judith. *Oya: In Praise of the Goddess*. Boston and London: Shambhala, 1987.

Gonzales, Patrisia. *Red Medicine: Traditional Indigenous Rites of Birthing and Healing*. Tucson: University of Arizona Press, 2012.

Goodison, Lucy, and Christine Morris, eds. *Ancient Goddesses*. London: British Museum Press, 1998.

Graulich, Michel. "Miccailhuitl: The Aztec Festivals of the Deceased." *Numen* 36, no. 1 (1989): 430–71.

Graulich, Michel, and J. de Durand-Forest. "On Paradise Lost in Central Mexico." *Current Anthropology* 25, no. 1 (1984): 134–35.

Graulich, Michel, Doris Heyden, Ulrich Köhler, Berthold Riese, Jacques Soustelle, Rudolf Van Zantwijk, Charles Wicke, and Karl Wipf. "Myths of Paradise Lost in Pre-Hispanic Central Mexico [and Comments and Reply]." *Current Anthropology* 24, no. 5 (1983): 575–88.

Graves, Robert. *The Transformations of Lucius: Otherwise Known as The Golden Ass*. New York: Farrar, Straus and Giroux, 1951.

Griffith, Ralph T. H., trans. *The Hymns of the Atharvaveda*. Benares, India: Lazarus, 1895–96. Available online at www.sacred-texts.com/hin/av/index.htm.

———, trans. *The Rig Veda*. Benares, India: Lazarus, 1896. Available online at www.sacred-texts.com/hin/rigveda/index.htm.

Guest, Lady Charlotte, trans. *The Mabinogion*. London: HarperCollins, 2000.

Harrington, Patricia. "Mother of Death, Mother of Rebirth: The Mexican Virgin of Guadalupe." *Journal of the American Academy of Religion* 56, no. 1 (1988): 25–50.

Harrison, Jane E. *Mythology and Monuments of Athens*. Whitefish, MT: Kessinger, 2004.

Harrison, Keith, trans. *Sir Gawain and the Green Knight*. New York: Oxford University Press, 1998.

Hartz, Paula R. *Native American Religions*. New York: Chelsea House, 2009.

Haskins, Susan. *Mary Magdalene: Myth and Metaphor*. Old Saybrook, CT: Konecky & Konecky, 1993.

Hebert, Jill M. *Morgan le Fay, Shapeshifter*. New York: Palgrave Macmillan, 2013.

Herskovits, Melville J. "African Gods and Catholic Saints in New World Negro Belief." *American Anthropologist*, n.s. 39, no. 4, part 1 (1937): 635–43.

Hesiod. *Theogony: Works and Days*. Translated by M. L. West. Oxford: Oxford University Press, 1999.

———. *The Theogony, Works and Days, and the Shield of Heracles*. Translated by Hugh G. Evelyn-White. New York: Dover, 2009.

Hiatt, L. R. "Swallowing and Regurgitation in Australian Myth and Rite." In *Australian Aboriginal Mythology: Essays in Honour of W. E. H. Stanner*. Edited by L. R. Hiatt, 143–62. Canberra: Australian Institute of Aboriginal Studies, 1975.

Higgins, Jean M. "The Myth of Eve: The Temptress." *Journal of the American Academy of Religion* 44, no. 4 (1976): 639–47.

Hirshfield, Jane, ed. *Women in Praise of the Sacred: 43 Centuries of Spiritual Poetry by Women*. New York: Harper Perennial, 1994.

Hollis, Susan Tower. "Women of Ancient Egypt and the Sky Goddess Nut." In *Special Issue: Folklore and Feminism*. Edited by Brvce Jackson. *Journal of American Folklore* 100, no. 398 (1987): 496–503.

Homer. *The Iliad*. Translated by E. V. Rieu. London: Penguin Books, 1950.

Horne, Charles F., ed. *Ancient Japanese Shinto Rituals to the Sun Goddess (Yengishiki)*. Whitefish, MT: Kessinger, 2006.

Hornung, Erik. *The Ancient Egyptian Books of the Afterlife*. Translated by David Lorton. New York: Cornell University Press, 1999.

———. *Der agyptische Mythos von der Himmelskuh: Eine Atiologie des Unvollkommenen*. Freiberg, Germany: Vandenhoeck & Ruprecht, 1982.

Huggens, Kim. *Complete Guide to Tarot Illuminati*. Woodbury, MN: Llewellyn, 2014.

———, ed. *From a Drop of Water: A Collection of Magickal Reflections on the Nature, Creatures, Uses and Symbolism of Water*. London: Avalonia Books, 2009.

———, ed. *Memento Mori: A Collection of Magickal and Mythological Perspectives on Death, Dying, Mortality and Beyond*. London: Avalonia Books, 2012.

———. *Tarot 101: Mastering the Art of Reading the Cards*. Woodbury, MN: Llewellyn, 2010.

———, ed. *Vs.: Duality and Conflict in Magick, Mythology and Paganism*. London: Avalonia Books, 2011.

Hulley, Charles E. *The Rainbow Serpent*. Sydney, Australia: New Holland, 1999.

Huysmans, J. K. *Against Nature*. Harmondsworth, UK: Penguin Books, 1975.

Hyde, Douglas. *A Literary History of Ireland*. London: Ernest Benn, 1967.

Imhoof-Blumer, Friedrich. "Griechische Münzen in dem königlichen Münzkabinet im Haag und in anderen Sammlungen." In: *Zeitschrift für Numismatik*. Band 3 (1876), S. 269–353

Isler, Martin. *Sticks, Stones, and Shadows: Building the Egyptian Pyramids*. Norman: University of Oklahoma Press, 2001.

Iwasaki, Michiko, and Barre Toelken. *Ghosts and the Japanese: Cultural Experiences in Japanese Death Legends*. Logan: Utah State University Press, 1994.

Janvier, Thomas A. *Legends of the City of Mexico*. New York: Harper & Bros., 1910.

Josephus, Flavius. *The Antiquities of the Jews*. Translated by William Whiston. Project Gutenberg [online], www.gutenberg.org/files/2848/2848-h/2848-h.htm.

Karcher, Stephen. *The Kuan Yin Oracle*. London: Time Warner, 2001.

Kaster, Joseph. *The Wisdom of Ancient Egypt*. London: Michael O'Mara Books, 1995.

Kato, Genchi, and Hikoshiro Hoshino, trans. *Kogoshui, or Gleanings from Ancient Matters*. Tokyo: Sanseido, 1926.

Keber, Eloise Quiñones. *Codex Telleriano-Remensis: Ritual, Divination, and History in a Pictorial Aztec Manuscript.* Austin: University of Texas Press, 1995.

Keightley, Thomas. *The Fairy Mythology: Illustrative of the Romance and Superstition of Various Countries.* London: H. G. Bohn, 1870. Available online at www.sacred-texts.com/neu/celt/tfm/index.htm.

Kerényi, Carl. *Eleusis: Archetypal Image of Mother and Daughter.* Princeton, NJ: Princeton University Press, 1967.

Key, Anne. "Tlazolteotl: The Goddess of Filth." *MatriFocus* 8, no. 3 (2009).

Klein, Cecelia F. "Teocuitlatl, 'Divine Excrement': The Significance of 'Holy Shit' in Ancient Mexico." In *Special Issue: Scatological Art.* Edited by Gabriel P. Weisberg. *Art Journal* 52, no. 3 (1993): 20–27.

Knight, Chris. "Levi Strauss and the Dragon: Mythologiques Reconsidered in Light of an Australian Aboriginal Myth." *Man*, n.s. 18, no. 1 (1983): 21–50.

———. "Menstrual Synchrony and the Rainbow Snake." In *Blood Magic: The Anthropology of Menstruation.* Edited by Thomas Buckley and Alma Gottlieb, 232–55. Berkeley: University of California Press, 1988.

Kramrisch, Stella. "The Indian Great Goddess." *History of Religions* 14, no. 4 (1975): 235–65.

Lacy, Norris J., ed. *Lancelot-Grail: The Old French Arthurian Vulgate and Post-Vulgate in Translation.* 5 vols. New York: Garland, 1993–96.

Larrington, Carolyne, ed. *The Feminist Companion to Mythology.* London: Pandora, 1992.

———. *King Arthur's Enchantresses: Morgan and Her Sisters in Arthurian Tradition.* New York: I. B. Tauris, 2006.

———, trans. *Poetic Edda.* New York: Oxford University Press, 1999.

Lawlor, Robert. *Voices of the First Day: Awakening in the Aboriginal Dreamtime.* Rochester, VT: Inner Traditions International, 1991.

Lele, Ócha'ni. *The Secrets of Afro-Cuban Divination.* Rochester, VT: Destiny Books, 2000.

Lewis, Mark Edward. *Flood Myths of Early China.* Albany: State University of New York Press, 2006.

Lichtheim, Miriam. *Ancient Egyptian Literature, Volume II: The New Kingdom.* Berkeley: University of California Press, 2006a.

———. *Ancient Egyptian Literature, Volume III: The Late Period.* Berkeley: University of California Press, 2006b.

Little, Stephen, and Shawn Eichman, eds. *Taoism and the Arts of China.* Chicago: Art Institute of Chicago, 2000.

Long, Asphodel P. *In a Chariot Drawn by Lions: The Search for the Female in Deity.* London: Women's Press, 1992.

Loomis, Roger S. "Morgain La Fee and the Celtic Goddesses." *Speculum* 20, no. 2 (1945): 183–203.

Lupak, Alan. *The Oxford Guide to Arthurian Literature and Legend.* New York: Oxford University Press, 2007.

Lynch, Patricia Ann. *Native American Mythology A to Z.* New York: Facts on File, 2004.

MacCurdy, George Grant. "An Aztec 'Calendar Stone' in Yale University Museum." *American Anthropologist*, n.s. 12, no. 4 (1910): 481–96.

MacDermot, Violet, trans. *The Fall of Sophia: A Gnostic Text on the Redemption of Universal Consciousness.* Great Barrington, MA: Lindisfarne Books, 2001.

MacKenzie, Donald. *Egyptian Myth and Legend.* London: Gresham, 1907.

Mair, A. W., trans. *The Complete Works of Callimachus*. East Sussex, UK: Delphi Classics, 2017.

———, trans. *Oppian, Colluthus and Tryphiodorus*. Loeb Classical Library 219. London: William Heinemann, 1928.

Mair, Victor, and Mark Bender. *The Columbia Anthology of Chinese Folk and Popular Literature (Translations from the Asian Classics)*. New York: Columbia University Press, 2011.

Marcos, Sylvia. "Indigenous Eroticism and Colonial Morality in Mexico: The Confession Manuals of New Spain." *Numen* 39, no. 2 (1992): 157–74.

Marquadt, Patricia A. "Hesiod's Ambiguous View of Women." *Classical Philology* 77, no. 4 (1982): 283–91.

Matthews, Caitlin. *King Arthur and the Goddess of the Land: The Divine Feminine in the Mabinogion*. Rochester, VT: Inner Traditions, 2002a.

———. *Mabon and the Guardians of Britain: Hero Myths in the Mabinogion*. Rochester, VT: Inner Traditions, 2002b.

———. *Sophia: Goddess of Wisdom, Bride of God*. Wheaton, IL: Quest Books, 2001.

McCall, Henrietta. *Mesopotamian Myths*. Austin: University of Texas Press, 1990.

McCarthy, F. D. "The String Figures of Yirrkala." In *Records of the American-Australian Scientific Expedition in Arnhem Land. Vol. 2, Anthropology and Nutrition*. Edited by C. P. Mountford, 415–511. Melbourne, Australia: Melbourne University Press, 1960.

McDaniel, June. *Offering Flowers, Feeding Skulls: Popular Goddess Worship in West Bengal*. New York: Oxford University Press, 2004.

McDowell, Bart. *Gypsies: Wanderers of the World*. Washington, DC: National Geographic Society, 1970.

McKlintock, Martha K. "Menstrual Synchrony and Suppression." *Nature* 299, no. 5282 (1971): 24–5.

Mead, G. R. S., trans. *Pistis Sophia: A Gnostic Gospel*. San Diego, CA: Book Tree, 2003.

Meador, Betty De Shong. *Uncursing the Dark: Treasures from the Underworld*. Wilmette, IL: Chiron, 1992.

Meeks, Dimitri, and Christine Favard-Meeks. *Daily Life of the Egyptian Gods*. London: Pimlico, 1999.

Mercer, A. B., trans. *The Pyramid Texts*. New York: Longmans, Green, 1952.

Milford, H. S., ed. *The Complete Works of William Cowper*. London: Henry Frowde, 1905.

Miller, Carol, and Guadalupe Rivera. *The Winged Prophet: From Hermes to Quetzalcoatl—an Introduction to Mesoamerican Deities through the Tarot*. York Beach, ME: Samuel Weiser, 1994.

Molina, Cristóbal de. *Accounts of the Fables and Rites of the Incas*. Translated and edited by Vania Smith-Oka and Gabriel E. Cantarutti. Austin: University of Texas Press, 2011.

Morenz, Siegfried. *Egyptian Religion*. Translated by Ann E. Keep. Ithaca, NY: Cornell University Press, 1973.

Motz, Lotte. *The Faces of the Goddess*. Oxford: Oxford University Press, 1997.

Mundkur, Balaji, Ralph Bolton, Charles E. Borden, Åke Hultkrantz, Erika Kaneko, David H. Kelley, William J. Kornfield, George A. Kubler, Harold Franklin McGee Jr., Yoshio Onuki, Mary Schubert, and John Tu Er-Wei. "The Cult of the Serpent in the Americas: Its Asian Background [and Comments and Reply]." *Current Anthropology* 17, no. 3 (1976): 429–55.

Murdoch, Brian O. *The Apocryphal Adam and Eve in Medieval Europe: Vernacular Translations and Adaptations of the Vita Adae et Evae*. Oxford: Oxford University Press, 2009.

Murdock, Maureen. *The Heroine's Journey*. Boston: Shambhala, 1991.

Murray, Robert. *Symbols of Church and Kingdom*. Cambridge, UK: Cambridge University Press, 1975.

Neginsky, Rosina. *Salome: The Image of a Woman Who Never Was*. Newcastle upon Tyne: Cambridge Scholars Publishing

Neumann, Erich. *Amor and Psyche: The Psychic Development of the Feminine; A Commentary on the Tale of Apuleius*. Translated by Ralph Manheim. New York: Pantheon, 1956.

Nonnus. *Dionysiaca*. 3 vols. Translated by W. H. D. Rouse. Loeb Classical Library. Cambridge, MA: Harvard University Press, 1989.

Norris, Frederick W. "Isis, Sarapis and Demeter in Antioch of Syria." *Harvard Theological Review* 75, no. 2 (1982): 189–207.

Núñez, José Corona. *Antigüedades de México: Basadas en la recopilación de Lord Kingsborough*. Vol. 1, *Colección Mendoza o Códice Mendocion: Códice Telleriano Remensis*. Facsimile edition with commentary. Mexico City: Secretaría de Hacienda y Crédito Público, 1964.

Obregón, Luis González. *The Streets of Mexico*. San Francisco: George Fields, 1937.

O'Neill, Joseph, trans. "Cath Boinde." *Eriu* 2 (1905): 173–85.

Ono, Sokyo, and William P. Woodard. *Shinto: The Kami Way*. Boston: Tuttle, 2003.

Ovid. *Metamorphoses*. Translated by A. D. Melville. Oxford: Oxford University Press, 1986.

Panayotakis, Costas. "Vision and Light in Apuleius' Tale of Psyche and Her Mysterious Husband." *Classical Quarterly*, n.s. 51, no. 2 (2001): 576–83.

Patai, Raphael. *The Hebrew Goddess*. Detroit: Wayne State University Press, 1990.

Pérez, Kristina. *The Myth of Morgan La Fey*. New York: Palgrave Macmillan, 2014.

Philostratus the Elder/Younger. *Imagines & Callistratus—Descriptions*. Translated by Arthur Fairbanks. London: William Heinemann, 1969.

Picard, David, and Mike Robinson. *Festivals, Tourism and Social Change: Remaking Worlds*. Clevedon, UK: Channel View, 2006.

Pintchman, Tracy. *The Rise of the Goddess in the Hindu Tradition*. Albany: State University of New York Press, 1994.

Plato. *Cratylus; Parmenides; Greater Hippias; Lesser Hippias*. Translated by Harold North Fowler. Loeb Classical Library 167. Cambridge, MA: Harvard University Press, 1926.

———. *Phaedrus*. Translated by Benjamin Jowett. New York: C. Scribner's Sons, 1871. Available online at www.sacred-texts.com/cla/plato/phaedrus.htm

———. *The Republic*. Translated by Paul Shorey. Loeb Classical Library. Cambridge, MA: Harvard University Press, 1930.

———. *The Statesman; Philebus; Ion*. Translated by Harold North Fowler and W. R. M. Lamb. Loeb Classical Library. Cambridge, MA: Harvard University Press, 1925.

Pritchard, James B., ed. *Ancient Near Eastern Texts Relating to the Old Testament*. Princeton, NJ: Princeton University Press, 1969.

Propertius. *Elegies*. Translated by G. P. Goold. Loeb Classical Library. Cambridge, MA: Harvard University Press, 1990.

Quintus Smyrnaeus. *The Fall of Troy*. Translated by Arthur S. Way. London: Barnes & Noble, 1995.

———. *The Fall of Troy*. Translated by Arthur S. Way. Milton Keynes, UK: Lightning Source UK, 2011.

Rabinowitz, Jacob. *The Rotting Goddess: The Origin of the Witch in Classical Antiquity's Demonization of Fertility Religion*. New York: Autonomedia, 1996.

Rasmussen, Knud. *Eskimo Folk-Tales*. Translated by W. Worster. London, 1921. [online] Available at www.sacred-texts.com/nam/inu/eft/index.htm

Reed, A. W. *Aboriginal Myths: Tales of the Dreamtime*. Sydney, Australia: New Holland, 2002.

———. *Aboriginal Tales of Australia*. Sydney, Australia: New Holland, 1998.

———. *Myths and Legends of Australia*. Sydney, Australia: A. H. and A. W. Reed, 1971.

Richter, Daniel S. "Plutarch on Isis and Osiris: Text, Cult, and Cultural Appropriation." *Transactions of the American Philological Association* 131, no. 1 (2001): 191–216.

Robinson, James M., ed. *The Nag Hammadi Library*. San Francisco: HarperCollins, 1990.

Robinson, Roland. *Aboriginal Myths and Legends*. Melbourne, Australia: Sun Books, 1966.

Rogers, Mary Eliza. *Domestic Life in Palestine*. Cincinnati: Poe & Hitchcock, 1865.

Rosenberg, Samual N. "Lancelot, Part III." In *Lancelot-Grail: The Old French Arthurian Vulgate and Post-Vulgate in Translation; Volume II*. Edited by J. Lacy Norris, 3–186. New York: Garland, 1993.

Ruether, Rosemary. *Goddesses and the Divine Feminine: A Western Religious History*. Berkeley: University of California Press, 2005.

Rundle-Clark, R. T. *Myth and Symbol in Ancient Egypt*. New York: Thames and Hudson, 1991.

Sadek, A. I. *Popular Religion in Egypt during the New Kingdom*. Hildesheimer Ägyptologische Beiträge 27. Hildesheim, Germany: Gerstenberg Verlag, 1987.

Schafer, Edward H. *The Divine Woman: Dragon Ladies and Rain Maidens in T'ang Literature*. Berkeley: University of California Press, 1973.

———. "The Jade Woman of Greatest Mystery." In *Special Issue: Current Perspectives in the Study of Chinese Religions. History of Religions* 17, no. 3-4 (1978): 387–98.

Schaup, Susanne. *Sophia: Aspects of the Divine Feminine Past & Present*. York Beach, ME: Nicolas-Hays, 1997.

Schiavo, Anthony P., Jr. *I Am a Christian: Authentic Accounts of Christian Martyrdom and Persecution from the Ancient Sources*. Merchantville, NJ: Arx, 2018.

Schipflinger, Thomas. *Sophia-Maria: A Holistic Vision of Creation*. York Beach, ME: Samuel Weiser, 1998.

Schipper, Kristofer. "Taoism: The Story of the Way." In *Taoism and the Arts of China*. Edited by Stephen Little and Shawn Eichman, 33–56. Chicago: Art Institute of Chicago, 2000.

———. *The Taoist Body*. Translated by Karen C. Duval. Berkeley: University of California Press, 1993.

Schroer, Silvia. *Wisdom Has Built Her House: Studies on the Figure of Sophia in the Bible*. Collegeville, MN: Liturgical Press, 2000.

Seneca. *Seneca's Tragedies VI: Hercules Furens, Troades, Medea, Hippolytus, Oedipus*. Translated by Frank Justus Miller. Whitefish, MT: Kessinger, 2010.

Sethe, Kurt. *Die altagyptischen Pyramidentexten*. Vols. I–II. Hildesheim, Germany: Georg Olms Verlagsbuchhandlung, 1908–10.

Shaw, Brent D. "The Passion of Perpetua." *Past & Present* 139 (May 1993): 3–45.

Siculus, Diodorus. *Library of History*. Vol. 3, Books 4.59–8. Translated by C. H. Oldfather. Loeb Classical Library. Cambridge, MA: Harvard University Press, 1939.

Sikes, E. E. "Nike and Athena Nike." *Classical Review* 9, no. 5 (1895): 280–83.

Spence, Lewis. *The Gods of Mexico*. New York: F. A. Stokes, 1923.

Sperling, Harry, and Maurice Simon. *The Zohar: An English Translation*. Vol. 1. London: Soncino, 1984.

Squire, Charles. *Celtic Myth and Legend: Poetry and Romance*. London: Gresham, 1905.

St. Teresa of Avila. *St. Teresa of Jesus, of the Order of Our Lady of Carmel*. Trans. David Lewis. London: Thomas Baker, 1904.

———. *Interior Castle*. Trans. E. Allison Peers. New York: Dover Thrift, 1946.

———. *Interior Castle* or *The Mansions*. Trans. B. Zimmerman. Minneapolis: Grand Rapids, 1911.

Staines, David, trans. *The Complete Romances of Chretien de Troyes*. Bloomington: Indiana University Press, 1990.

Stern, David, and Mark Jay Mirsky. *Rabbinic Fantasies: Imaginative Narratives from Classical Hebrew Literature*. Yale Judaica. Philadelphia: Jewish Publication Society, 1990.

Stokes, Whitley. *Goidelica: Old and Early-Middle-Irish Glosses, Prose and Verse*. London: Trübner, 1872.

Sullivan, Thelma D. "Tlazolteotl-Ixcuina: The Great Spinner and Weaver." In *The Art and Iconography of Late Post-Classic Central Mexico*. Edited by Elizabeth Hill Boone, 7–36. Washington, DC: Dumbarton Oaks, 1982.

Tacitus, Publius Cornelius. *The Annals of Imperial Rome*. Translated by Michael Grant. New York: Penguin Classics, 2003.

Taylor, Thomas, trans. *The Hymns of Orpheus*. London: T. Payne, 1792. Available online at www.sacred-texts.com/cla/hoo/index.htm.

Teish, Luisah. *Jambalaya: The Natural Woman's Book*. New York: HarperCollins, 1985.

Torquemada, Fray Juan de. *Monarquia Indiana*. 3 vols. Mexico City: Porrua, 1969.

Trible, Phyllis. "Depatriarchalizing the Biblical Tradition." *Journal of the American Academy of Religion* 41 (1973): 30–48.

Turville-Petre, E. O. G. *Myth and Religion of the North: The Religion of Ancient Scandinavia*. New York: Holt, Rinehart and Winston, 1964.

van der Toorn, Karel, Bob Becking, and Pieter van der Horst, eds. *Dictionary of Deities and Demons in the Bible*. Leiden, The Netherlands: Brill, 1999.

Versluis, Arthur. *Wisdom's Book: The Sophia Anthology*. St. Paul, MN: Paragon House, 2000.

Wade, James. *Fairies in Medieval Romance*. New York: Palgrave Macmillan, 2011.

Waida, Manabu. "Sacred Kingship in Japan." *History of Religions* 15, no. 4 (1976): 319–42.

Waley, Arthur D. "Hymns to Kuan-Yin." *Bulletin of the School of Oriental Studies, University of London* 1, no. 3 (1920): 145–46.

Walker, Sheila S. "Everyday and Esoteric Reality in the Afro-Brazilian Candomble." *History of Religions* 30, no. 2 (1990): 103–28.

Walter, Mariko Namba, and Eva Jane Neumann Fridman, eds. *Shamanism: An Encyclopedia of World Beliefs, Practices, and Culture*. Santa Barbara, CA: ABC-CLIO, 2004.

Warner, W. L. *A Black Civilization*. New York: Harper, 1957.

Werner, E. T. C. *Myths and Legends of China*. London and Bombay: George G. Harrap, 1922.

Wilkins, W. J. *Hindu Mythology, Vedic and Puranic*. London: W. Thacker, 1900.

Williams, Ellen Reeder. "Isis Pelagia and a Roman Marble Matrix from the Athenian Agora." *Hesperia* 54, no. 2 (1985): 109–19.

Willson, Martin. *In Praise of Tara: Songs to the Saviouress*. Boston: Wisdom, 1996.

Wolkstein, Diane, and Samuel Noah Kramer. *Inanna: Queen of Heaven and Earth*. New York: Harper & Row, 1983.

Wright, Thomas. *Songs and Carols from a Manuscript in the British Museum of the Fifteenth Century*. London: T. Richards, 1856.

Wu Hung. "Mapping Early Taoist Art: The Visual Culture of Wudoumi Dao." In *Taoism and the Arts of China*. Edited by Stephen Little and Shawn Eichman, 77–94. Chicago: Art Institute of Chicago, 2000.

ABOUT THE AUTHOR

Kim Huggens's first Tarot deck, *Sol Invictus: The God Tarot*, was published in 2007, and her first book, *Tarot 101: Mastering the Art of Reading the Cards*, came out in 2010. Later, she worked with artist Erik C. Dunne to create the bestselling *Tarot Illuminati*, and together they worked on a sister deck, *Tarot Apokalypsis*. Kim's passion for Tarot is matched by her passion for mythology, and she has edited three anthologies exploring mythological themes: *From a Drop of Water*, *Vs*, and *Memento Mori*. She completed postgraduate studies in ancient history, focusing on the magic and religion of the classical and late antique world. Kim lives in Wales, United Kingdom, with her partner and black cat.

ABOUT THE ILLUSTRATOR

Following the publication of *Sol Invictus: The God Tarot*, **Nic Phillips** almost immediately began work on this deck with Kim, while also expanding his artwork into different media on a larger scale. With a keen interest in the folklore of the British Isles, he wrote and illustrated *Celtic Saints of Western Britain* and moved to live and work in Glastonbury, United Kingdom, surrounded by its Arthurian history and esoteric mystery, where he produces spiritual and Goddess-themed artwork. Nic's other research interests include world mythology and the nature of pilgrimage, and he is also currently working on a book about the Black Madonna.